MIRAFLORES

Memoir of a Young Spy

MIRAFLORES

MEMOIR OF A YOUNG SPY

KEITH YOCUM

ISBN 978-0-9978708-7-9
eISBN 978-0-9978708-6-2

This is a work of fiction. Names, characters, businesses, places, events and incidents are either the products of the author's imagination or used in a fictitious manner.

Cover design and typesetting by Stewart A. Williams

Again, and always, for Denise

FORWARD

Nicholas (Nick) Haliday, an employee of the Central Intelligence Agency for more than thirty-six years, died in 2008 at the age of seventy-three. He was predeceased by his wife Eleanor by two years.

While cleaning out his belongings, Haliday's two adult children discovered an unpublished, typewritten memoir titled "Miraflores" in a folder buried in the back of their father's filing cabinet. The date on the manuscript is June 1970. Their father never mentioned the existence of the memoir, which describes his first assignment for the agency in Panama in 1958.

After reading the manuscript, the children retained a lawyer, who contacted the CIA seeking permission to publish the manuscript. After repeated requests and a lengthy wait of nearly a decade, the agency returned the memoir with minor redactions.

The children agreed that their father's story would disadvantage no one who is alive today. They are proud of his service to the country and recognize that there are no saints in that business, just sinners with varying degrees of complicity.

CHAPTER 1

I was seventeen years old when my mother killed herself.

She was an alcoholic and died at home from an overdose of Placidyl and vodka, while I sat daydreaming in my high school English class.

It's easier to write this long after she died. Time acts like the slow drip of water in a subterranean cavern to soften those sharp, rocky emotions. This much is clear now.

But at the time of her death, my adolescent brain was doing what adolescent brains do: muddle the strange external world with internal volcanic emotions. So, with no other likely candidates, I blamed my father for my mother's death.

That sour relationship with my father led me — of all things — to a career as a spy in our country's intelligence service. To this day, my calamitous first assignment in Central America seems gauzy and unreal, as if it happened to someone else. Anyone but me — a confused, angry, and fragile young man whose job was to save the Panama Canal, the entire thirty-seven mile long ditch that we stole fair and square many years before.

And, strangely, it all started with my mother's death. Stick with me; it's a tale that I'm both proud of and humiliated by.

The day she died, Mrs. Riley, the headmaster's secretary, interrupted English class and whispered to my teacher. I watched as both sets of eyes swiveled like tank turrets until they settled on me. I couldn't figure out what I'd done wrong and it didn't take long for my classmates to follow the adults' eyes. Several giggled in anticipation of some fabulous punishment coming my way. The infraction had to be something high on the private-school infraction scale for the headmaster's secretary to interrupt a class.

"Nick, would you please follow me to the office," Mrs. Riley said. "And bring your things with you."

The "bring-your-things-part" was not a good sign. My friend Dave said in a very loud whisper, "I'll write you in prison." There was a smattering of chuckles, but I should have known something was wrong when Mr. Mandrake, the English teacher, said, "Shut up, David."

It wasn't Mandrake's manner to snap at students, especially at a snotty private school like St. Mark's in Washington, D.C.

Mrs. Riley said nothing as we walked down the cold, empty hallway, our steps bouncing sharply off the metal lockers that stood like a frowning gauntlet. I began to panic because she was typically a warm, pleasant, adult and her behavior at that moment was oddly distant.

She walked hurriedly a few steps ahead of me as if she preferred to not see me. When we swept into the office, the other adults raised their eyes to look at me, then looked away. I was confused by all of this and remember furiously trying to guess what I had done wrong.

"Nick, why don't you go into the headmaster's office?" Mrs. Riley said. "He's waiting for you."

Pausing only slightly, I walked right into Mr. Negosian's office. He was sitting at his desk writing something. He looked up and flashed a smile, though it was gone in a millisecond.

"Nick," he said, "could you close the door?"

I swung the huge solid-oak door shut, hearing it click solidly into place like a bank vault. He gestured for me to come over to his desk and told me to put down my books.

"Nick, there's been an accident in your family, and you need to call home. Here's the phone."

"OK," I said, feeling a mixture of relief and embarrassment. My face and neck flushed.

As soon as Negosian mentioned "accident," I knew it was my mother. Her drinking was so extreme that she sometimes fell and hurt herself, or she would drop and shatter a glass, cutting her feet in the process. As an only child with a busy and mostly absent father, taking care of mother fell to me and to our loyal maid Elma.

One time mother fell out of bed late at night and hit her head on the corner of the bedside table. My father was on another of his long overseas trips, so Elma and I cleaned up mother the best we could. But she bled a lot. In the end, she needed five stitches to close the gash.

For days afterwards, she would delicately touch the tiny black stitches with her fingertips as if she were a blind person inspecting a stranger's face.

So, I assumed that mother had another one of those accidents.

I dialed the headmaster's rotary phone, watching each number mechanically return to its starting place. I waited while my home line rang four times. Then, instead of Elma answering, my father answered.

"Hello," he said in a tone that was a half-octave higher than normal.

"Father, this is Nick," I said. "Headmaster Negosian told me I should call home. He said there's been an accident."

"There's been a terrible accident, Nick." He paused for several seconds and I could hear him breathe into the mouthpiece. "Your mother is dead. She died early this afternoon."

I bit my bottom lip, which was a nervous habit that I still have, and raised my eyes to look at Negosian. But he had his head down, writing something to avoid eye contact. I panned the headmaster's office, taking in the pictures on his wall showing ceremonial grip-and-grin photos of school benefactors, Glee Club members, and groundbreakings.

In fact, there were so many of these pictures on his walls that I followed them around like a trail of breadcrumbs. My reverie was interrupted by my father.

"Nick?"

"Uh huh."

"I'm sending my driver to pick you up. Could you please hand the phone to Mr. Negosian?"

"My father wants to talk to you," I said, handing the heavy black Bakelite handset to the headmaster.

It was difficult to know what they talked about because Negosian didn't say much. He nodded a lot and said things like, "absolutely," "that will not be a problem," and "certainly."

After he hung up, Negosian looked at me for a second and said, "Nick, I'm very sorry to hear about your mother's passing. Please accept the condolences of everyone at St. Mark's. I'm sure you're in a state of shock at the suddenness of this — this tragedy." He shook his head back and forth and sighed deeply. "Your father has a driver on the way over here. I'd like you to just sit in that chair there and we'll let you know when he arrives."

My father's drivers were always changing so I didn't know this guy. I remember he kept glancing in the rearview mirror of that cavernous car to look at me. I kept busy by counting the number of fire hydrants we passed.

And I thought of my poor mother. At this point, I didn't know the nature of the "accident," so I tried to conjure up how she might have died. It seemed like an uncaring thing to do at that moment, but when you have an alcoholic parent, well, you spend your life expecting bad things. And you grow numb, which is perhaps the worst part.

To be honest, Elma and I often worried that mother would drown in the bathtub, because she insisted on soaking there with a book, a martini, an ashtray, and her pack of Viceroy cigarettes. She would put her "goodies," as she called them, on the wicker clothes hamper that she would pull over to the tub. Elma scolded mother for doing this, but of course, she couldn't stop her.

One evening I heard Elma scream; then I heard a loud thump upstairs that shook the floor. I ran up to find Elma pounding on my mother's back as she lay face down on the floor of the bathroom, her hair matted over her face. Mother was covered only partly with a big towel that Elma had thrown over her back.

"Mrs. Haliday!" Elma screamed. "Wake up. Wake up!"

Seeing me wide-eyed — I was in the seventh grade at the time — Elma said, "Nicky, call the ambulance. Your mom drowned!"

But just then mother coughed and spit up what seemed like a gallon of water. She moaned, raised her head, and looked toward the doorway where I was standing. Her dark wet hair stuck to her face like a pile of seaweed. As she rose up on her elbows, I saw her breasts, bone white and cylindrical. Seeing that really bothered me.

Driving home from school, I was convinced she drowned in the bathtub. In truth, I was so confused and stunned that I could only concentrate on that stupid bathtub.

We pulled in front of the house, and the State Department driver tried to open the door for me, but I jumped out lugging a pile of books under my arm. There was a police car in front and another car that I didn't recognize.

I walked in the front door and heard voices in the living room and was about to go in there when I froze. I stood in the hallway for several minutes, listening to the muffled voices when I heard Elma yell as she spied me from the kitchen, "Good heavens, Nicky!" She ran over and smothered me with a hug.

The awful realization of my mother's death was starting to worm its way into my consciousness, as hard as I tried to avoid it. I felt a strange mixture of dread, relief, embarrassment, anger, and sadness.

So, I cried.

Well, it was more of a loud whimper. But all those confusing years of embarrassment and anger around my mother's alcoholism were swirling near the surface. I dropped my books when I couldn't hold them any longer. My father came running out of the living room and he hugged Elma and me.

We made a silly kind of scene — an adult sandwich with me in the middle surrounded by the two slices of bread — my father and Elma, our Black housekeeper.

After a minute or so we broke up, and my father asked me to go with Elma into the kitchen while he finished talking to the police. As he turned to reenter the living room, I peeked and saw two policemen in uniform sitting uncomfortably on the couch, their silver badges sparkling in the light.

Elma made a sandwich for me and poured a glass of milk, but I couldn't eat. I sipped at the milk.

"Poor Nicky," she kept muttering to herself. "Poor Mrs. Haliday."

At this point, I was just trying to figure out what to do. I had no idea how to act or behave. My mind was blank. "Poor Mother," I kept repeating to myself. "Why did she have to fall asleep in that stupid bathtub? Damn her."

CHAPTER 2

My father and I didn't get along.

You might think he was a mean person, or a distracted professional not keen on fatherhood. But you'd be wrong.

The biggest issue was that we didn't know each other. He traveled often on long, important trips for the State Department. For much of my childhood, we lived overseas. When I was in elementary school the constant moves didn't seem to bother me. But in junior high, I began to hate the moves.

I don't remember my mother drinking when I was younger, but by the time I was in eighth grade in the American School in Berlin, I noticed her strange speech patterns in the evenings. I began to associate the slurring with her love of martinis. My father also started to confront her about her drinking, and they sometimes argued.

Perhaps my relationship with my father would have been better if I had siblings. But it was just the three of us. My father tried his best to engage me, but I felt so much closer to my mom. And I began to resent him being away from home so much. Somehow — I'm not sure exactly how this happened — but I began to feel that my father was to blame for my mother's drinking. And this blame sat there below the surface of our relationship like an unmarked navigational hazard, ready to make profound mischief for the unwary mariner.

My father used to call me "Nickle" sometimes instead of Nick. I suppose it was a form of endearment, but it just pissed me off.

"Hey, Nickle, how's school going?"

"I don't know, Father, OK I guess." To be fair, when I was younger, I didn't actually *hate* him.

It was the letter that made me despise him.

The morning after my mother's death lots of people came to the house to visit. The cars were everywhere, and Elma was so flustered she started talking to herself. "How will I ever keep up? Impossible!" I helped her make sandwiches; carefully cutting the crusts off them when she was finished. Then we filled small sparkling crystal bowls with pickles and olives. It kept me occupied.

People, especially my aunts, would come in and just look at me and sigh. Then they'd walk away teary eyed. I felt like a sad old panda bear in a zoo that people were staring at. It also embarrassed me because they knew about my mother's alcoholic "accident." It's funny, but at this moment I was more embarrassed than sad about my mom's death, which says a lot about the strange thinking patterns of children of alcoholic parents.

Some of my cousins came too, including Kathy Haliday, Uncle Bob and Martha's daughter. I thought she was kind of cute, but she was just a ninth grader. We stared at each other and drank Nehi orange soda. What could you say to a ninth grader?

"I'm really sorry about your mom," she said.

"Me too," I said.

"I know she's in heaven looking down on you right now," Kathy said earnestly.

"I just hope she's sober," I said, taking a big gulp of the fizzy orange liquid.

That wasn't the best thing to say under those circumstances and poor Kathy just looked at me with those big brown eyes.

"Oh," she said and got up and left.

I saw her whispering to Aunt Martha across the room and I quickly left the room in retreat.

In the late afternoon, after everyone left, Elma cleaned up, and I watched TV by myself in the den. It was a classic formulaic episode of Lassie. That dog was brilliant, and I could never figure out how Lassie knew who had fallen down a mineshaft, or that there was a cougar lurking in the barn. Even though I was a senior in high school, you have to remember this was the 1950s when life was simpler — mountain lions: bad; Lassie: good.

My father came over and sat next to me. He patted my head and stood up to turn off the TV. I kept looking at the screen. Those old black-and-white picture tubes would collapse to a white dot about the size of pencil eraser after you turned them off, and the dot would stay there for maybe thirty seconds. I just kept staring at the white dot; it seemed like a burning white star tugging me with its gravitational field.

"Nick, I need to talk to you," my father said.

"Uh huh," I said.

"You need to look at me. You're seventeen years old and we need to have a serious discussion."

I did not like the sound of that.

"Nick, we have to talk about your mother."

"Uh huh."

"Nick, look at me," though, to be honest, I thought I was.

"Your mother died at around 11:30 in the morning. She died in the bedroom."

"I thought she died in the bathtub?"

"Who told you that?"

"No one. I just guessed it, that's all."

"Well, she didn't die in the bathtub. She died in her bed. Now I've thought a lot about this, and while several folks, especially some of your aunts, don't think you should know all the details, I believe you're old enough to know the truth."

I finally looked at him, unnerved by the direction the conversation was taking.

"Your mother had a drinking problem and you know that. Heck, I suspect you know more about it than I do." He turned his head and looked out the window into the yard. I followed his gaze and watched our neighbor's calico cat stalk a bug across the cement walkway.

Sighing, he turned back and said, "And while I've been counseled by some to fib to you about your mother's death, it just doesn't seem right to do so. You're a young man and you deserve the truth." I quickly shot a glance at the TV, hoping the white dot was still there, but it was gone.

"Your mother was also unhappy, Nick. She was depressed. And the drinking made things worse. Your mother was also having trouble sleeping, and she was seeing a psychiatrist. She convinced her doctor to give her sleeping pills. And well, she took too many pills yesterday, Nick. And she drank an awful lot of vodka too."

"Oh."

"And she died when the alcohol combined with the sleeping pills. She fell off the bed and got sick on the floor, but by the time Elma arrived she had stopped breathing. There was nothing that could be done."

I stared over my father's shoulder so I wouldn't have to look him in the eye. One of my mother's favorite paintings hung on the opposite wall, so I just stared at it, feeling strange and disconnected.

"Nick, are you listening to me?"

"Yep." But I was busy trying to think of something else, something far away.

"Nick. This is important. Your mother did not die accidentally. It was on purpose."

"On purpose?" I asked slowly.

"Yes."

"What do you mean?"

"She meant to end her life, Nick. She was profoundly unhappy and ill."

Have you ever been struck on the head completely out of the blue? It happened to me in baseball practice once. Chris Wells, our third baseman for the JV team, was standing behind taking practice swings with a bat. I stepped backwards not realizing he was there and took the Louisville Slugger on the right side of my skull. One moment I was daydreaming and sucking on a blade of grass and the next I was on the ground eye to eye with Chris's cleats and a towering forest of grass. The accident happened so fast that I was utterly disoriented.

That's how I felt when my father told me that my mom died "on purpose." It was very, very confusing. I felt dizzy and reached out to put my left hand on the coffee table. What could he possibly mean by "on purpose?" I just stared at him, looking for some clue that would help me decipher what he had just said.

We stared at each other for a while. Then he swallowed hard — I could see his Adam's apple move about two inches vertically — and said, "She was in a lot of emotional pain, Nick, and I'm absolutely certain that if she could, she would take it all back in a second. But she can't. None of us can."

"What do you mean 'on purpose'?" I asked, suddenly feeling angry.

"She did it to herself. She wanted to end it, Nick."

"How do you know? It was an accident. I bet she didn't know what she was doing! You know how she got sometimes."

"It was on purpose, Nick."

"What the hell are you talking about?" I yelled.

"Nick, it was not an accident. We know that."

"That isn't true!" I said standing up. I think this is where I started to cry.

"Nick, it's OK. It's not a good time right now. Let's talk about this later."

"No! I want to know what you're talking about. How can you say Mother died on purpose? That's suicide! Mom would never do that! You're crazy! It was an accident, and I can't believe you think she would do that! You're so blind."

"There was a note, Nick."

I snuffled myself together, feeling the salty tears run over the top of my lip and into my mouth.

"What note? What are you talking about?"

"She left a note."

"A note?"

"Yes. She wrote a note telling me what she was doing."

"I don't believe it," I yelled. "You're making this up!"

"We'll talk in the morning, Nick. Let's get some sleep. I'm exhausted. I can barely think."

"I want to see the note," I said, though in truth I didn't really want to see it.

"It was written to me, Nick. I don't want to show it. It was private."

"You're making all this up! She would never kill herself!" I spluttered. "You're just covering up the fact that you messed up her life! You made her sad! You're the one that kept moving us around. You were never home. It's your fault!"

Up to this point, I knew I was out of control, screaming and choking through my tears. But as soon as this last part tumbled out of my mouth, I took a shocked breath. I couldn't believe what I said.

My father's eyes widened and for a second I thought he was going to hit me. I even think I flinched.

Then he said coldly, "Sit down."

But I didn't sit down. He was wearing a gray suit with a white shirt and dark blue tie. He reached inside his suit coat and pulled out a single piece of vanilla-colored paper. It was my mother's fancy notepaper. It had a thick blue stripe all around the border and was milled with a jagged edge. She used to write my school notes of absence with that paper.

He just looked ahead at the cold, ash-filled fireplace in front of him and held the note out to me.

I stared at the piece of folded paper but didn't touch it

"Go ahead. Read it," he said flatly.

After a few seconds, I reached over and reluctantly took the folded piece of paper in my fingers. A sheet of paper never felt so heavy.

CHAPTER 3

"Dear Phil,

It is better this way, and you know it. I can't go on. Life is so complicated. I will miss Nick so and I'm afraid he'll never understand. Will anyone?

Margaret"

I read the letter and was shocked at how little she said. My first thought was that it was a fake — I was busy trying to do anything to protect myself from the truth — but it was mother's writing, though it was sloppy.

I reread the letter several times, especially the sentence where she said she'd miss me. Of course, I wouldn't understand. How could I understand what just happened? And each time I read the five sentences, something happened inside me, like a bellows on a coal fire; each pass of the letter was like a huge puff of hot air that made the coals shine brighter and hotter. I was building up a wave of astonishing anger toward my father. When I put down the letter — I didn't hand it to him — I was enraged.

Let me try to explain something. My mother embarrassed me deeply. I was ashamed of her and openly hostile at times. When I was younger, I had no idea she was an alcoholic, so her behavior was perplexing, but not upsetting. As I got older, my school friend Felix asked me about my mother and her "problem." I didn't understand, and when I pressed him, he just shrugged. I asked my father about her slurring once when I was eleven — we were living in Hong Kong then, and he was really upset. My parents got in a big fight afterward, and I think my mother's "problem" got better. For a while.

When I was thirteen, we took an ocean liner back to the US from Hong Kong. We stopped everywhere in the Pacific, and I was happy that there was an Australian boy named Alex also on board. We had a ball.

Except that mother's "problem" was worse. She stayed in our cabin all the time and just lay in bed. One day Alex and I stopped by our cabin, and my father was there with the purser. My mother was sitting up with her legs on the floor. Her hair was a mess and her back bent as she stared at the floor.

"Nick, why don't you and Alex go swimming?" my father said.

"Sure," I replied. "Hey, Mom, how are you feeling?" She didn't respond. I could smell alcohol everywhere.

"Here is some more," the purser said, pulling down two bottles of vodka from a compartment above my bunk bed. He put them next to three empty bottles.

"Is your mum sick?" Alex asked.

"Yep," I said.

"Get going, Nick, please," father said.

I grabbed my trunks and left. Alex and I did cannonballs off the small diving board. Then we pretended to be underwater frogmen on a secret mission. Only the pool was filled with saltwater and it hurt our eyes. Meanwhile, though, I was furious at my mother, and I don't think I spoke to her for a full three days. By then she was sober, and she acted as if nothing had happened.

And just like that, I stopped being mad at her.

About a week later we steamed into Pago Pago in American Samoa for a day of sightseeing. The island looked like a volcano with a thick green carpet laid over its contours. And as we inched into the deep harbor, I stood on the promenade deck with my parents. I was struck by the extraordinary beauty of this volcanic outcropping jutting out of the Pacific Ocean. Having the three of us together again felt great.

But my mother went sightseeing with some friends, ditched them and found a bar on the island, where she got really, really drunk. My father raced to find her before the boat left. He was really pissed off. The rest of the trip back to San Francisco, he wouldn't let her leave the ship at any port of call. He made the cabin attendant keep an eye on her when he was out walking around the ship.

The strange thing is that my mother really pissed me off and I hated the embarrassment she caused me. But guess what? I chose to dislike my father more. He was always traveling. Even when we were stationed overseas, he was never home. Plus, he just wasn't warm to me like mother was. He seemed awkward. So, somewhere deep inside my teen-age brain, even though my mother was the cause of more grief and embarrassment in one week than my father created his whole life, I chose to blame him for everything. Especially in my role as the only sober family member around to look after her.

The moment I read her suicide note that evening, all the anger I had inside me focused on my father, not my mother. There was no logic to this clumsy narrative I constructed, but there you have it.

When I put down the letter in the living room that night, I was still standing while my father sat staring into the empty fireplace. He normally had a commanding bearing, with his shoulders set square and his back ramrod straight. But that night he was bent forward, his hair disheveled and his tie slightly off-center.

I could barely control myself with my swirling anger. And I already missed my mother, though in truth I missed my sober mother, not my drunk mother.

"I hate you. You're the one that killed her."

Behind me, I heard Elma yelp. I didn't realize she was nearby.

When I turned, I saw an awful look on her face. Her eyes were already red from crying, and she looked exhausted, holding a tray of little sandwiches and glasses of milk.

"Don't say that, Nicky," she said, breaking with emotion. "Please don't talk that way."

I was too far gone to care.

"He killed her, Elma!"

"No, Nicky," she said. "Stop it." And then she ran from the room, the glasses clinking precariously on the tray. I heard her crying in the kitchen.

My father cleared his throat, sighed deeply, and then said evenly, "I'm going to take Elma home. I'll be gone for about thirty minutes. You should get some sleep. There will be many more guests tomorrow."

With that, he stood up, grabbed the letter off the table, and left. I heard him trying to comfort Elma, but she just kept crying in the kitchen. After they left through the kitchen door, I slowly made it to my room. At the top of the stairs, I realized that my mother had just died on the floor of the room next to mine, and I panicked: I was the only one in the house at this moment and I was scared.

I walked slowly to my parents' bedroom. I suppose I expected it to look different or at the very least to have a white outline of the body on the floor, like in a silly detective show.

But there was nothing different about the room. My mother's clothes and jewelry were in the same place; the stockings were still draped over the door of her armoire. I walked slowly around the room, my heart thumping loudly as if I was trespassing into a forbidden area. Then I walked lightly over to the side of the bed my mother slept on.

And there, on the carpet, about three feet from the bed was a dried white patch on the blue carpet. Leaning over I could see that it had been hastily wiped up but not vigorously cleaned. It was the last thing my mom did while she was alive.

Vomit.

CHAPTER 4

Perhaps the best way to describe the relationship with my father after my mother's death was as a type of Cold War: there were brief periods of détente, but mostly there was subterfuge and sabotage on my end, with an occasional outbreak of open hostilities.

The funeral was a big deal. I really didn't know my father was so important at the State Department. There were important people everywhere in boat-sized, black Cadillacs, including Secretary of State John Foster Dulles. I didn't know who Dulles was, but my cousin Kathy — who appeared to have forgiven me for being a jerk a couple of days earlier — fingered him at the graveside.

"Nick, my mother says that old guy over there is the Secretary of State," she whispered. "I think those are his bodyguards standing next to him. Neat, huh?"

"I guess."

"And that man over there with the big nose? He's a senator, but I don't know his name."

"Really?"

"Yep. This is fanciest funeral I've ever been to."

"Yeah, me too."

But of course, it was my mother they were burying, so things were strange all around. When you're young and one of your parents dies, well, the best way to describe it is that it's like sitting submerged on the bottom of a crowded swimming pool — you can watch kids play tag above you, adults swim laps on the surface, and divers knife into the water at the deep end. But at the same time, you're aware of an overpowering sense of self-awareness. Your heartbeat is amplified, you can hear the tiniest bubbles slip past your ear, and your whole being seems to be under a magnifying glass.

I survived the funeral and the reception at the house afterwards. I slinked away with Kathy and my thirteen-year-old cousin Greg and played ping pong in the basement. Back and forth we banged that ball until we couldn't stand it anymore. Then we played some 45 rpm records that I had on a record player. Kathy and Neil liked "Doggie in the Window" by Patti Page, and they made me play it three times in a row.

And one by one our guests left until it was just father, Elma, and I. No mother.

Now you would think that the outpouring of grief and sympathy for my mother's death by all these important people would have made me feel better, but it didn't. I was interested in only one thing — making sure my father knew that he was responsible for my mother's death.

Also, I had trouble feeling sad, just embarrassed. But two months after my mother died, I was taking a shower before school, and as I stood under the deluge of hot water I was suddenly overcome by a profound sense of grief. Maybe it was the water that coaxed the tears out, but I just started sobbing uncontrollably, my right arm held up against the green tiles in the shower as a rest for my forehead.

Things were strained around the house afterwards. My father said he was not going to travel so that he could be at home. We were civil, though everything had changed, of course. I didn't have to take care of mother, and Elma really didn't have much to do either.

My mother died on March 12, 1953, during my senior year at St. Mark's. I was only out of school for about a week because there wasn't much use moping around the house.

Applying to college in those days was much simpler. I applied to only two schools and was accepted at Georgetown University, my number one choice. Before I knew it, I was at the senior prom dancing the night away with Debbie McIntyre, my sometimes girlfriend. To be honest, I have only one memory of the graduation ceremony: walking up to the podium to accept my fake diploma from Mr. Negosian and noticing that Bill Sims who was walking ahead of me had put his gown on backwards. That's my only memory of graduation.

Father hosted a small family graduation party at the house. All my uncles and aunts made polite comments about how proud they were of me, about how my mother would be proud of me. I felt uncomfortable about the overflow of pity, and I slinked away with my cousins and played tag football in the yard.

That summer I took up the same summer job I'd had the past two years as a lifeguard at the country club.

In July my father took me aside one evening.

"Nick, I need to talk to you before you go out tonight," he said.

"Can't it wait? Timmy and I are going to a movie."

"It's important. Please just sit down for a few minutes."

I sat down in the kitchen and did my best to look bored.

"In just about a month you'll start living away from home for most of the year, albeit just down the road. I've thought long and hard about whether we need to live in this huge house. I was wondering how you would feel about moving?"

"Moving? Where?"

"I thought about buying a townhouse in Georgetown. I'd be closer to work and you could drop over any time you wanted."

I was shocked that he wanted to sell the house. Maybe he wasn't crazy about all the memories that went with it.

I feigned a lack of interest in the whole idea, which was my preferred approach to my father in those days.

Looking at him that evening in the kitchen, I noticed that his hair was grayer than I had ever seen it. And his bearing seemed stooped, his face haggard.

He sighed and looked down at the linoleum floor, then raised his head.

"Nick, I know you don't want to hear this, but I miss your mother. This house reminds me too much of her and I think it's best if we start anew, you and I."

"Sure," I said, with about as much enthusiasm as someone about to have a cavity drilled.

"And I need to get more involved with work. Probably more assignments overseas again. I don't know how much you read the papers, Nick, but this is a very difficult time for the department. There is a senator who's making accusations about State Department employees and it's caused quite a ruckus. The FBI has been investigating everyone. It's disgraceful what's going on. But no one seems to be able to stop it."

"The FBI?" I asked, now curious. "Are they investigating you?"

"Perhaps. I'm not sure. None of us knows. I guess I'm not worried, though I've seen other innocent people caught up in this tragedy."

"What do they think you've done?"

"They're looking for communists, Nick. This crazy senator says there are communists in the State Department, and he wants to root them out."

"Does he think you're a communist?"

"He doesn't know who I am, but he's got the FBI looking into the backgrounds of every department employee, so you never know what they'll turn up. But no, Nick, I'm not a communist nor will they find anything on me. It's still a travesty."

"Oh," I said.

"But I also want to talk to you about Elma. I don't think we need her any longer. Once we move, I don't think I'll need a housekeeper since I may be out of the country for long periods."

"Oh," is all I could muster. "What will Elma do?"

"Hopefully, she'll get another job. She's terrific and will get a stellar recommendation from me. But don't worry, I'll take care of her financially so that if she wants, she won't have to work again."

"Gee, I'm going to miss her," I said.

"Yes, me too. She's a wonderful person."

CHAPTER 5

Georgetown University sits atop a rocky outcropping in the southwest corner of Washington, DC. Looking out my dorm window I could see the languid Potomac River below and the tony suburb of McLean on the Virginia side. And of course, Georgetown was a school full of white kids with rich and powerful parents.

It's a Catholic school and Jesuits ran the place. If you know anything about the Jesuits, you know how brilliant and loopy they are. Like a lot of Catholic universities, Georgetown has since become less Catholic, but in the 1950s it had a strong religious underpinning. Priests were plentiful and most students had them as academic advisors. Father O'Malley, an intense little red-faced Irishman, was my advisor.

I don't think he liked being a priest because he hated wearing his collar and gown. And he never wanted to talk about academics or religion, just baseball and politics.

He was particularly upset with the Washington Senators baseball team and could not understand how a team in the nation's capital could be so inept. In September 1954 the Senators set a team record by losing their one-hundredth game of the season. Father O'Malley was nearly suicidal.

"For God's sake, why is it necessary to punish these fans? What have they done?" he complained in one of our sessions. "It's not fair, Nick, to humiliate such a proud town. This is not Sodom!"

I kind of felt sorry for the poor guy, but he was inconsolable. Besides, Washington was Sodom to me, as you'll see. Father O'Malley tried to talk me into attending a game with him at Griffith Stadium to see the Yankees, but I demurred. I was afraid he'd scream at the players for the entire game.

Originally, I wanted to go to Georgetown because mother convinced me that I could have a rewarding career in the Foreign Service. I think she liked the idea that I might follow in my father's footsteps, though I don't know why because she hated all the traveling. To be honest, she probably thought my father could help me along into a fabulous career. She was smart about things like that.

And Georgetown had an excellent International Affairs Department, so it seemed obvious that I would gravitate towards that discipline. Dr. Wilson, the chair of the department, really sucked up to me whenever he could. He said he was a friend of my father's and was interested in making sure I was comfortable at Georgetown. You can imagine that's about all it took to turn me away from majoring in International Affairs.

In the 1950s people still wrote letters, and my father wrote letters to me about once a week. I wrote back sporadically. At this point, he was back on the road again and was stationed in Tokyo for my entire sophomore year. He begged me to visit him, but I thought it was too far and I was too busy.

Well, busy is probably too mild — I was going wild.

I had discovered beer and girls, in that order. Nearly every weekend there was a party at someone's house — including my father's townhouse. He had left a key to the place, and I put it to good use. Some Sunday mornings there were beer cans and ashtrays on every conceivable flat surface in the house. Guys and even some girls were strewn over the three floors of the townhouse.

In those days a girl was seen to be "loose" if she had sex with a guy, so there weren't many girls who stayed over. But several stayed late, sometimes until dawn.

That's where I met my first serious flame, a student at George Washington University named Naomi Stern. She was brash, self-confident, and Jewish. She was also beautiful. One Saturday evening she showed up with a group of GW girls at one of my townhouse parties and man, did she make her presence known.

We sometimes sat around at these parties and had spirited debates about everything from Mickey Mantle to communism and the free world. If there were any girls in attendance they'd sit around the edge and watch the guys show off their alcohol-dulled debating skills. It was old-fashioned and chauvinistic, but as I said, this was 1955, and it was a different world.

The first night I met Naomi she sat on the outside of the group of testosterone-driven male debaters. She watched as Fred Foster and this guy I barely knew named Carl Johansson went toe-to-toe on whether Senator Joseph McCarthy was a devil or a saint. The previous year the US Senate had censored McCarthy and pretty much ended his career.

Still, some people thought he was right and that a vast communist conspiracy had penetrated this country and the administration of President Dwight Eisenhower.

"So, you think there are no communists in this country right now, trying to undermine our government, weaken our resolve?" Foster said, baiting Johansson.

"I didn't say that. I'm just suggesting that there's no proof that there were communists in the State Department, and precious little proof that there are communists anywhere in this government," Johansson said.

"Why do you need proof?" Foster shot back. "There's no proof there isn't a conspiracy either. McCarthy was trying to warn us that we shouldn't be complacent."

"Don't be stupid. We don't need false accusations in order to rouse us from complacency," Johansson said.

"But you don't know there's *not* a conspiracy afoot in this country," Foster persisted. "How can you be so sure he wasn't right?"

And then, from the back of the small crowd, came Naomi's voice piercing clear: "For the same reason I know that you're drunk. You keep repeating the same solipsistic nonsense. None of McCarthy's State Department charges were ever proven true, yet you keep saying they could be true. If proof that someone's accusations were false is not proof enough for you, then no one can ever win an argument with you."

"Precisely," Johansson said laughing. "That's my point."

Fred was not so much thrown off by Naomi's logic, but by the fact that it came from a woman.

The group roared with laughter as Johansson hid behind Naomi's argument and Fred stood stunned, peering into the back to see who he was up against.

"Let's play some music, Nicko," someone yelled.

"Yeah," others chimed in, and that was the end of that Great Debate. I put on some 45's and tried to find out who that girl was.

But she found me. I was standing in the kitchen and had just finished puncturing the second triangular hole in a beer can when I heard a voice behind me say, "So how does a Georgetown undergrad rate an entire townhouse to himself? You must be loaded."

"Oh," I said turning to see her grinning. "Well, it's not mine. It's my father's and he's overseas right now. So, I thought I'd use it for educational purposes."

"What makes you think he's not on his way home right now from the airport?" she said.

"Mmm, hadn't really thought of that," I said, smiling at this confident, funny girl. "I guess I'm putting my faith in the power of a benevolent god to allow these educational sessions to continue. I believe in a merciful god, as you can see."

"I believe in a vengeful god," she said, taking a sip of beer.

"Yipes, that's kind of a dark view of things," I said. I found myself liking this verbal sparring. It was new to me and frankly kind of titillating.

"It's a pragmatic view," she said. "It keeps me from getting caught."

"Ha," I said. "Maybe that's why I keep finding my fair share of infractions at school."

"You Catholics spend your lives punishing yourselves. You revel in guilt."

"We do?"

"Of course. You're probably feeling guilty right now that you're using your dad's pad for this party and that you're not studying for your English Lit final."

"I hadn't thought about it, but now that you mention it, I'm feeling a trifle guilty," I laughed.

"You know why we Jews don't suffer as much guilt?" she asked, taking another sip of beer.

Mesmerized by the conversation I couldn't help but let her lead me. "No, why?"

"Because we go right to the source, we cut out the middleman. My relationship with God is between him and me. You Catholics have to go through your priests — they're your middlemen. They keep reminding you about how guilty you should be."

"Jeeze, I guess I never thought of it that way," I said shaking my head in amazement. "Makes me want to become a Jew."

"Don't go rushing into that too quickly," she said with perfect sarcastic pitch. "You may have your priests, but we have our mothers. I'll take the priests any day."

When I stopped laughing, she smiled and said, "Nice house. Thanks for letting us crash your party." Then she turned and left the kitchen.

"Hey wait," I yelled. "What's your name? I don't even know who you are."

She stopped. "My name's Naomi. What's yours?"

"Nick."

"Nick," she repeated. "That's a short, perfunctory name."

"It was given to me, what can I say!"

I pursued Naomi relentlessly afterwards. She thought it was "cute" that her little "goy friend" was interested in dating her. She was such a breath of fresh air compared to the other girls I had met in college. At first, I had been put off by her brashness, but after a while, it grew on me. I also discovered that it was a ploy on her part; she was insecure, just like the rest of us. Still, Naomi was such a wonderful girl and not afraid of taking life head on.

CHAPTER 6

Naomi and I dated for the rest of my sophomore year — she was a freshman — and through my junior year. During the summers we wrote lots of letters to each other and spoke on the phone. She lived in New York City. Her father was a cardiologist, and I gather a pretty accomplished one at that. At least that's how she presented it.

She also told me her parents were upset that she wasn't dating a Jew. In the end, that issue sunk our relationship. For all Naomi's brashness and remarkable self-assurance, she couldn't endure by her parents' displeasure.

We tried not to let that stuff bother us during the school year. Her GW dorm had a stringent curfew, and we did our best to hang out between schoolwork and her holidays at home.

Though we dated for quite a while, we never actually had sex, though I tried mightily. We made out a lot in my car and on the couch in my father's townhouse, and she tolerated a fair amount of "petting," as it was delicately referred to back then. She had the most wonderful, firm breasts and sometimes would let me get my hands underneath the monstrous bra she wore. It seemed to cover her entire stomach.

And every now and then she would get so worked up that she would make little panting noises and powerful, guttural sighs. She would let me rub my open hand against the front of her underwear but under no circumstances could any of my digits get past the rim of her underwear elastic. Invariably she would collect herself during these petting sessions and say, "Stop Nick."

And I would, though it would leave me with an enormous erection I could not hide. Naomi used to laugh at me.

"Jeeze, Nick, your bean stalk need trimming."

"Well, I know how you can trim it," I would banter.

"Go trim it yourself," she would say. "Or is that a sin for you Catholics?"

"It's a mortal sin. I can go to hell forever if I die without going to confession first."

"Of course," she would say, fixing her dress. "Why would it be any other way? Eternal damnation for self-gratification. Makes perfect sense."

Like I said, she was an accomplished tease. And had great breasts.

And yes, I was a virgin when I graduated from college in May 1957. Just ask Naomi.

The relationship with my father was moribund. He began to travel again and was not around. And even when he was in town, I had trouble warming to him.

He tried to make our situation better. He wrote long, impassioned letters about issues the United States faced in the world. These letters impressed me with their thoughtfulness and articulation. I had a grudging respect for his patriotism and moral compass. He was a spirited fighter in this crazy, dangerous period of the Cold War.

But of course, I had my own Cold War going on at home. My father figured out but never gave up trying to fix it. He attempted to be part of my life by meeting my friends and bantering with them. He even took Naomi and me out to dinner at fancy restaurants in Washington. Naomi thought my father was very suave, handsome, and looked like Cary Grant. She could not understand why I was not close to him.

"Nick, you're crazy," she said to me in April of my senior year. I remember we were walking languidly around the Tidal Basin next to the Jefferson Memorial. The cherry trees were in full bloom and an idle breeze loosened a soft fragrant blizzard of pink petals. I was feeling romantic, but Naomi kept pressing me on my feelings for my father. She seemed agitated by our relationship.

"But don't you think that it's time to loosen up with your dad? Do you really think he was entirely at fault for your mom's death? And even if he was absent because of his job, he really doesn't seem like he meant to hurt anyone. Jeeze, Nick, he's a heck of a lot nicer than my father."

"Do we really have to talk about this stuff?" I said. "Isn't this a beautiful day? Can you smell blossoms?"

"Nick, you're frustrating to talk to sometimes. Did anyone ever tell you that?"

"No. Just you and my father."

"Mmm. Now that I think of it, maybe you're just frightened of intimacy."

"Good grief! Now you're talking like Sigmund Freud. They're filling your head with too much junk at GW."

"Like I said, Nick, you need to loosen up with your dad."

"Don't call him 'Dad.' I never call him that."

"More evidence for my diagnosis."

"Ugh, Naomi. Can't we just walk? You're giving me a headache."

So, we held hands and sashayed like young lovers twice around the basin. It was a wonderful day; I fantasized about Naomi and me getting married and having wild sex every night. It was fun to dream.

The idea to join the CIA emerged out of the blue in my senior year. It was the first semester and we had an English teacher named Father Simonescu. While he was certainly bright like most Jesuits, he was also batty, like most Jesuits. He had a nervous tic that every thirty seconds or so would contort the side of his face. I think we all felt awful for the poor guy, but as the semester wore on it was too painful to watch him in front of the class, so I doodled or stared out the window onto the Georgetown neighborhood.

And one day, sitting in Father Simonescu's class, I started doodling on my notebook while mulling the question of what I was going to do upon graduation. Some of my friends were going on to law school. One of them was in pre-med, but most were just going to disperse back to their hometowns and look for work there. I really didn't have a hometown, though the Washington, D.C. area would have to suffice. My father had been pestering me about what I intended to do and recommended I consider the State Department.

Of course, that was the last thing I wanted to do. The State Department stood as the catalyst for my mother's death: it yanked my father away from home, made my mother bored and lonely, which in turn led her to drink and eventually kill herself. That was my simple math back then about the dynamics of our family relationships.

As I doodled that day in class, I drew a large letter "C" and created a shadow box for the "C" so that it looked three-dimensional. It was my normal method of doodling in which I would embellish letters and words with flourishes and then look up dutifully at Father Simonescu in mock abject concentration and note taking as he droned and twitched on.

On this particular day, doodling away and staring out onto rooftops in congested Georgetown, it suddenly occurred to me that my father despised the CIA. I knew this because he had sometimes vented to my mother at the dinner table about problems he'd had at work. When we were in Hong Kong, for instance, he was very upset about something that happened in the embassy. I was just a kid, so I didn't really understand what he was talking about.

"Margaret," he said, digging into his dinner plate, "it's just preposterous that they can simply come in and undermine all that we've done.

We had a perfectly good working relationship with this man Chang, and he was a reliable back channel into the mainland. And now this. Unbelievable!"

"Are you sure the CIA was involved?" my mother asked. "It could have been anyone."

"They admitted it to us!" he said. "The station chief told the ambassador himself. They were working this same source, unbeknownst to us. And they compromised him. Said it was an 'accident.' Just unbelievable! And who do they answer to? None of us has any idea who oversees that group of rogues and thieves. They can just show up, set up shop, push their own agenda, and do whatever they want. It's absurd."

"Philip, you really shouldn't let those people upset you," my mother said. "Besides, they seem like a force to be reckoned with. Perhaps you should seek out the station chief. Try to befriend him. He might be helpful in your career. They sound like powerful people."

"Good grief, Margaret," he said. "They're unprincipled. They're thieves and liars. I'd rather befriend the devil first!"

"Philip," she said, "you should try not to let these things bother you. You're all on the same team."

"The CIA is on no one's team," my father said, putting down his fork.

At this point, I couldn't resist, and I jumped in. "What's the CIA?"

"See?" my mom said, "You've got Nick all in a dither now."

"The CIA," my father said, measuring his words precisely and looking at my mother briefly, "is a government agency. It stands for the Central Intelligence Agency. They're basically spies, I guess. And, well, sometimes they come into contact with us in the State Department. And, I suppose, we have good-natured disagreements. But your mother is correct, Nick, we're all on the same team."

"Spies?" I said. "That sounds really neat. Do they carry guns?"

My father frowned at that and said, "Not all of them, Nick. Just a few. Most of them are just office people. Like me."

I tried to engage him in more conversation about spies but he would have none of it. And I pretty much forgot about the CIA until the last year of my mom's life. Once, at the dinner table again, my father was extremely agitated about the investigations of State Department employees by the FBI. This was during the McCarthy period and he was about as angry as I've ever seen him in my life.

"They're going through every record and every contact any of us have *ever* had with a communist. It's a witch hunt, Margaret. And you have no idea what they'll come up with or manufacture! It's those bastards at CIA and FBI who are running roughshod over everyone."

"Philip, watch your language," my mother said. "Nick doesn't need to hear this."

"Oh mom," I told her, "this isn't so terrible. You ought to hear how the kids talk at school."

And this comment started my mother off on one of her rambling diatribes against the lack of morals she saw in young kids today. I think she had been drinking most of the day at this point, so it was kind of embarrassing to watch her make a fuss out of something so small.

But I never forgot, I suppose, that my father hated the CIA. Sitting in class that day I slowly drew the letter "I" and followed it with an "A."

Was I trying to punish my father, or take a stand against the State Department, the organization that took him away from our home? Or was I simply looking for an exotic, exciting career that would take me away from my home? I had no idea.

CHAPTER 7

It was not easy to apply to the CIA in those days. I searched through the Georgetown library looking for an address or a phone number, but I could find nothing. I even called directory assistance out of desperation.

"We don't have a listing for the Central Intelligence Agency," the operator told me.

"How about just 'CIA'?"

"No, sir. No listing there either."

"How about the Office of Strategic Services?" — I read this was their name during World War II. It was a stretch.

"No, sir."

"Well, how about the FBI — the Federal Bureau of Investigation? Can I have their number?"

"I have that one, here you are."

I was a determined little Boy Scout and figured the FBI knew the phone number of the CIA.

The operator at the FBI said she had no idea what I was talking about and pretended not to have heard of the Central Intelligence Agency.

"You know," I persisted, "they're the agency that runs our spy services overseas. You must have heard of them?"

"Umm, maybe I have," she said. "Can I have your name please?"

Even in my near perfect state of ignorance, there was something odd in her voice, so I became suspicious.

"Jeeze, can't I just talk to someone at the CIA?" I said.

"Let me see if I can help," she said. "Please hold."

After what seemed like fifteen minutes of dead time, a man with a deep voice came on the line.

"Hello, can I help you?" he said.

"Yes, I'm looking for the phone number of the CIA. Do you have it? I can't seem to find it anywhere."

"We might be able to find it for you, but I would need to look it up and call you back. Can I get your phone number and perhaps your name?"

The guy sounded so official and commanding that I nearly gave it to him without thinking. And yet there was something unsettling about the exchange and I had the strangest feeling that I was being manipulated. Paranoia ran rampant in those days. I hesitated, and the man pressed ahead, feeling my reluctance.

"Don't worry," he said. "I should be able to call you back today."

At that point, it occurred to me in a rush of anxiety that he was only interested in identifying me, and I did the only thing a self-respecting, frightened college kid could do — I hung up.

A week later a couple of us seniors were sitting around someone's dorm when one of my friends Rich — a long-distance runner on the Georgetown track team — bragged about a letter he received recently. It was a recruiting letter from a government agency asking him if he was "interested in serving his country in the battle against Communism?" The letter stated that it was an exciting life involving overseas deployment and defending the United States against a worldwide conspiracy.

"But who sent it?" my friend Steve asked, holding the letter in his hands. "There's no identification of the government agency that sent it. Just a phone number on the bottom. Kind of weird if you ask me."

I took the letter from him and read it closely as the others talked. While there was no letterhead or other identifying marks it sounded official. The letter never stated that the type of work they were recruiting for involved clandestine activities, yet it was implied somehow.

"I bet this is from the CIA," I said. "In fact, I'm sure of it."

"The CIA?" Rich said. "Jeeze, that's the spy agency, isn't it? Wow. A spy. I could be a spy."

"Maybe it's just the Army," Steve said. "Maybe they're trying to trick you into enlisting with the Army. I don't think spy agencies send letters like this to recruit spies. Doesn't that sound stupid?"

"Mmm," Rich said, "that does sound crazy. Maybe it's the FBI?"

"They don't normally deploy overseas," I said. "It's the CIA, not the Army or FBI. Why don't you give them a call to find out?"

Everyone in the room looked at Rich.

"I'm not going to call the CIA," he said. "They'll put me on a list if I'm not interested. I'll be black-balled the rest of my life for any job I apply for."

"Yeah," Steve said. "I wouldn't call. Just throw it away."

I walked across the room to Rich's desk, picked up a scrap of paper and a pencil and copied the phone number at the bottom of the letter.

"Hey, what are you doing?" Rich said.

"I'm writing down the phone number. I'm going to find out who sent this. Maybe I'd like to join the CIA one day."

"But it was addressed to me," Rich said. "I'll get in trouble if they think I gave the number out to other people. This is serious, Nick. Don't get me in trouble."

"Jeeze, Rich, calm down. If you received this letter, then a lot of other guys have got letters too. It's probably just a single phone number to call. I'll never mention you, don't worry."

"Come on, Nick," Rich said. "This whole thing is kind of spooking me. I don't think you should call them."

"Don't be so paranoid," I laughed. "Senator McCarthy's washed up, remember? Relax."

Yet, I was spooked by the idea of interacting with the CIA. I'm not sure whether it was all the drama around Senator McCarthy and his hearings, the "worldwide Communist menace," or the constant threat of a nuclear World War III, but it was natural to be paranoid in the 1950s.

I decided to make the call from a phone booth on campus. There was a bank of booths in the student union and I picked one out that was bookended by empty booths. I dropped a handful of coins on the stainless steel mini-table top and closed the hinged glass door. The light overhead came on and the fan started up. I spread the small piece of paper with the phone number on the table next to the coins and studied it for a minute in the weak light of the booth.

I had a nagging feeling that I was doing something wrong. The letter was not addressed to me. If they wanted to recruit me, they could have sent me a letter, but they didn't. Also, while I suspected it was the CIA, in truth it could have been the Army or any of the services. The Korean War had ended five years earlier. While we weren't at war, it seemed the world was in constant turmoil from the Hungarian Revolt to the Suez Canal Crisis.

But I was impelled by this youthful desire to join the CIA and I dialed the number.

"Hello?"

"Um, I was responding to a letter about a job for the government. It had a phone number on it."

"I see."

"Is this the right number? Did I misdial?"

"No," the man said. "This is the right number."

"Um, OK," I said.

"When did you receive the letter?"

"Well, I didn't actually receive the letter."

"You didn't? How's that?"

"My friend got the letter and I took the phone number down and decided to call."

There was a pause. I could hear the man's breath on the receiver. It was slow and measured. As I waited for a response I began to panic. Perhaps this was a bad idea after all.

"What's your friend's name?"

"Um, I'd prefer not to give it. I don't want to get him in trouble."

"Well, I'd need to know his name so we can keep track of the letters. This is official business."

This caught me off guard. I thought I'd be able to talk to the recruiter and find out about the job without divulging anything. And I promised Rich not to use his name. But I also wanted to know if this was the CIA and I felt tantalizingly close to finding out.

We all have character traits — some we like, some we don't. I had developed a defensive brashness when I was trapped. I was not sure whether it was innate, or I learned it from my mother, but it was there, nevertheless.

When I was a senior at St. Mark's, a group of us skipped school one spring day and went to an amusement park nearby in Maryland. Feeling brash, we didn't change out of school uniforms. The next day the senior class was called to a special assembly where Mr. Negosian the headmaster announced somberly that several boys from St. Mark's had been seen at the amusement park the previous day by a patron of the school.

Negosian went on to say that the patron was certain the delinquent boys were seniors. "We have a list of all the seniors who missed school yesterday, and before we interview all of you, we're going to give you one chance to come clean in front of your classmates. Those seniors who skipped school yesterday and visited the amusement park, please come to the front."

I shot a quick glance at my friend Danny and he grimaced. I looked farther down the line of seniors and caught the eye of another delinquent named Dave, and he raised his shoulders as if to say, "What should we do?"

After it was clear that no one was going to turn themselves in, Negosian sighed dramatically and said, "Well then, if that's the way it's going to be, will the following boys stay after the assembly —"

I found myself standing and interrupting him. "Sir?" I yelled.

"What is it, Nick?" Negosian said. Nearly every neck in the gymnasium turned in my direction as if it were a tennis match and the white fuzzy ball was bouncing toward me.

"Sir, I don't mean any disrespect to the patron, but how could they be certain the boys were from St. Mark's? There are many private schools in the area."

Negosian peered at me sharply and said, "Well, Nick, don't you think a patron would recognize the St. Mark's uniform?"

"Um, well, sir, we all know that Bishop Feehan has an almost identical uniform. Why couldn't it be that the 'delinquents' were from Bishop Feehan? Why should some of the boys here have to pay for something done by the boys at Feehan?"

Several boys nearby said "Yeah!" and the gymnasium broke out in loud mummering. I agree it was a silly thing for me to do, really. I had no idea what force impelled me to be so audacious. But there it was.

"With all due respect, sir, wouldn't it be better if the patron could be contacted to make sure that it wasn't those kids at Feehan that are getting us in trouble? Sir."

The crowd of seniors buzzed and nodded their heads. I sneaked a quick look at Dave, and he rolled his eyes in utter disbelief.

But the fact is Negosian turned to Father Samuelson, the assistant headmaster, and conferred with him for a moment.

Then he quieted the class down by raising his hand.

"OK, Nick, that is probably not a bad idea, though I doubt the patron — who I know personally and can vouch for — is capable of misidentifying St. Mark's uniform. For the sake of accuracy and fairness, we will check with the patron."

Either through pure luck or fatigue on Negosian's part with the year ending, the senior class was never called back to turn over their scofflaws.

I explain this because the same boldness took hold of me that day, on the phone to an unnamed official at a mysterious government agency trying to corner me into giving up the name of the kid who shared his recruitment letter. I wasn't sure whether Rich was at risk of being reprimanded, but it wasn't right to give up his name.

"So, in order to go on with this conversation, we need to know the kid's name who we sent this letter to," the man insisted, his voice hardening.

"Well, let's face it. That's not really important," I replied. "You guys must have sent hundreds of these letters out and many of them were never even answered, so finding out who shared his letter with me couldn't be that important."

I have no idea why I said that or how I figured out on the fly that in fact, they must have sent out lots of these letters, and at least in Rich's letter, there was no demand that the letter be responded to.

The man did not answer right away, but I distinctly heard his heavy breathing above the annoying sound of the phone booth fan. I waited for him to speak, which by itself was brash, while I watched students walk by outside the booth on their way to class. In an odd way, I was charged up by this cat-and-mouse interchange with a faceless government official.

"OK," he finally said. "Then how about *your* name? Are you authorized to give me your name?" His sarcasm had a tinge of anger in it, but

I decided to just plow ahead anyway.

"Sure. It's Nick Haliday." I spelled out the last name because some people spell it "Holiday."

"Well, Nick," he said, "did you say you were in college?"

"Yes, sir. Georgetown University. In Washington, D.C."

"What year are you in?"

"I'm a senior. I'll be done in just a month or so."

"Do you have a phone number and a home address?"

I gave it to him, and before I could ask him a question — like what government agency was recruiting — he ended the conversation perfunctorily with "We'll contact you if we're interested in pursuing this further." And he hung up.

CHAPTER 8

In my senior year at Georgetown, I still lived on campus, though I could have easily lived at my father's townhouse. I guess it was really our home and not just a weekend party pad for me and the guys.

My father never pressed me on why I preferred to remain on campus; he just let it be. It's not that I considered the townhouse "enemy territory" or anything so crass or obvious. It just seemed to me that we had sold our family home, and with my mother gone, it didn't seem like a true family any longer.

When he was back in town — which seemed to be for two weeks or so at a time — my father made it a habit to see me as much as he could. I started to like him. He was bright, articulate, and genuinely interested in my life.

Yet I still didn't trust my feelings. Later, I recognized that this trait was common among so-called Army brats, State Department children, and the children of missionaries. We kids all shared the same rootless, ex-pat existence. The isolation and relentless forced separation from familiar schools and friends created a distinct personality. We were self-sufficient, insecure, emotionally hardened, and worldly. We rode an undercurrent of suppressed anger and cynicism, mostly directed at our parents, but any authority figure would do nicely.

During my father's brief visits, he would often invite me over to the State Department cafeteria. One day he said right out of the blue: "Do you miss your mother as much as I do?"

"Yes, of course," I said. We never really talked about mother, since the bruises were still deep and painful — for both of us.

"Well, I really miss her," he said, toying with his macaroni and cheese. "Sometimes I wish we could just return to life like it was before. You know, all three of us and Elma. Living in that big house." He sighed. Perhaps it was the light in the cafeteria, but the corners of his eyes were fissured with deep wrinkles.

I felt sorry for him — and for me. But I had trained myself early on to avoid direct access to painful emotions.

I said, "Me too," and let the sadness dissipate in the clinking of plates and happy nearby lunchtime chatter.

It was no surprise that I didn't know my father very well. I had no idea what he did during the evenings when he came back stateside, what books he read, who he had dinner with, what he thought of the Washington Redskins, and things like that. For that matter, I didn't know what his life was like overseas — I think he was in Japan during this period.

I was afraid to know him, I suppose, because people I liked always went away. Some, like my mother, disappeared for good.

The letter was addressed to "Mr. Nicholas Haliday" and looked very impressive. The envelope was made of a heavy grade vanilla-colored paper. The return address was a post office box in Washington, D.C.

"Dear Mr. Haliday,

Thank you for your interest in working for one of the most important and exciting United States government agencies. We have received many responses to our recruitment letters and would like to invite you to learn more about this opportunity."

The letter went on to provide a date and time, but no address, for this "introductory session." There was a phone number to RSVP and receive "travel details." The agency doing the recruiting was never identified, but to me, there was no mystery.

My father had no idea what I was up to. He asked me several times what I was going to do after graduation. I was vague and non-committal.

"Have you thought about law school?" he asked me one evening right before he returned to Tokyo after the Christmas holidays. "You're a very smart young man. You'd do well in law, Nick. You should consider it."

"Sounds kind of boring," I said.

"Nothing wrong with 'boring,'" he replied. "There are some very fine careers that may appear 'boring'. You should consider it."

"To be honest, I was looking for something more exciting and challenging," I said.

"Like what?"

"I don't know, maybe something to do with international relations."

"You mean the State Department?" he said brightening. "Is that what you mean? That's very exciting work, Nick. We need good people who get the big picture and understand how complex our relationships are with the rest of the world. This is great news!"

My father rarely showed raw enthusiasm. He was, I guess, a good bureaucrat — taciturn, serious, reserved, and competent. But this evening his face lit up as he thought I was announcing my interest in following in his footsteps.

"Nick," he said leaning toward me across the small round dining-room table, "you probably don't want to hear this, but your mother was hoping you would consider the State Department. It's a noble profession."

Seeing him so animated I felt guilty with this cat-and-mouse game. His eyes were wide with suppressed excitement, and he fiddled with his hands as he bubbled with ideas on my entry into the State Department. I stared at him for several minutes as he talked about who I should contact to network, what books I should try to get hold of, and the like.

"Actually, I was thinking of another kind of foreign service. I mean, I have nothing against the State Department," I said.

He stopped, looked confused, then smiled slowly. "You mean you're interested in a humanitarian agency, like AID, CARE or the United Nations? Something like that? Gee, Nick, I guess I never pegged you for someone interested in that kind of work. That's a wonderful calling."

"Well, maybe. I'm still just thinking of all my options. Sorry if it's unformed at this point."

"Not at all, Nick," he said. "I guess I'm pushing you and I don't mean to. It's just the parent in me." He laughed.

The next morning, he left early. I heard the driver helping him with his suitcases. It was interesting to hear them act so deferential to him: "Can I carry that, Mr. Haliday?" "Is this bag going as well, Mr. Haliday?"

There were about eighty of us, mostly men but there was a smattering of women. Everyone looked young and painfully earnest.

The small auditorium was inside one of two nondescript structures called the "Munitions Building." They were built quickly during World War I and sat on Constitution Avenue in Washington, D.C., near the Lincoln Memorial.

You can't find these buildings any longer because President Richard Nixon ordered them torn down in 1970. Until they tore the ugly things down, I couldn't pass these buildings without feeling a small spasm of anxiety.

★

The fact that the Munitions Building belonged to the US Navy was baffling and caused a bit of panic. If the CIA hosted this recruitment meeting, why would they meet in a Navy building? Was the US Navy recruiting us?

I heard several other participants grumbling as well, so I was not alone in my disappointment.

We filed into a small amphitheater and sat nervously while we waited. I chatted amiably with the fellow sitting to my left. Perhaps in the spirit of the mystery surrounding the meeting, neither of us divulged too much personal information. But it was clear to me that he was also taken aback by the venue.

"This is a Navy building," I said.

"Yes," he said, nodding. "Very interesting."

"It's not what I expected," I said.

"Me either," he said.

And just as the murmuring in the crowd began to rise to a low roar, we saw a man walk to the podium. There was a large microphone on a stand and he played with it for a second. The crowd quieted.

"Welcome," the man said. "My name is Fred Whitley. Thank you for joining us today. Please take a second to look around you. Yes, go ahead, take a second to glance around." I thought it was a bit melodramatic, but I dutifully looked around like everyone else.

You are looking at the cream of the crop of the American university system," he continued. "Many of you were at the top or near the top of your classes; many of you are top athletes. In fact, several of you represented the United States in the '56 Olympics. You are the best that this country offers in terms of education, physical strength, and patriotism."

As Whitley spoke a palpable sense of self-assurance permeated the room. I found myself slowly enthralled by him; he seemed urbane, worldly, well spoken, and profoundly self-confident. He wore a blue, pinstriped wool suit, a starched white shirt, and a red-and-blue striped tie. He had jet-black hair, with touches of gray at his temples. He looked to be in his early fifties, though he could have been much older.

And his insistence that we were the very best this country had to offer was intoxicating. During his speech I suddenly found myself perching forward on my seat, uncontrollably trying to get closer to him.

"Now, I am aware that many of you are uncertain what government agency is interested in recruiting you. It is the same agency that I have devoted myself to for many years in the cause of freedom. It is the Central Intelligence Agency, though doubtless, you may have already guessed that much. We are in fact in a hiring mode, since we have many, many challenges throughout the world today. This is our largest 'freshman class,' as it were, and our friends at the Navy Department have graciously agreed to let us use this room."

Whitley spoke for about forty-five minutes, and I confess to being enthralled by his description of the challenges the United States faced on so many fronts. The most pressing issue, he returned to over and over again, was the "worldwide Communist conspiracy" to convert fledgling democracies and even dictatorships to Marxist/Leninist totalitarian regimes controlled from Moscow or Peking.

To emphasize this point Whitley walked away from the podium and approached a huge map of the world. Although he was now out of the range of the microphone, his voice was clear and resonant. He pointed to a spot on the map that I could not see.

"Vietnam: a country occupied brutally by the Japanese in World War II and nurtured by the French before and after, now has a communist insurgency funded directly by the Chinese." He moved his hand and pointed to another spot on the map: "Malaysia: a Chinese-backed communist insurgency is threatening to unseat the British, who have had to resettle almost half-a-million people in a bid to isolate the rebels." He moved again: "The Philippines: a communist insurrection among agrarian groups in Central Luzon that is showing signs of worsening."

And he went on from continent to continent citing endless examples of communism's attempt to hide behind the goal of "peaceful co-existence." I must admit, hearing him speak and watching him move around the world from Vietnam to Nicaragua to the Eastern Bloc was frightening and unnerving.

Finishing his map exercise, Whitley returned to the podium.

"And this is where you come in. We need freedom fighters, men — and women — who are willing to take the fight to communists in their own backyards. It's a fight that is not conventional. We don't sit in opposing trenches lobbing artillery shells at each other until one of us gives up. Not on your life! It's much more subtle and secretive — but just as dangerous. Make no mistake about it; this is a real war. And we need your help. It's as simple as that. If we can't stop them, well then" — he turned with a great flourish and pointed at the map — "the entire map will be red one day. All of it, including the People's Republic of Nebraska. Mark my words."

Then, bowing his head slightly in what I took as a kind of salute to the eighty or so in the audience, Whitley said quietly, "Thank you. And God bless."

Well, I certainly wasn't the first to stand up to lead the thunderous ovation, but I wasn't far behind. There were no tears of patriotism in my eyes, but I was sorely tempted. He was that good and I so desperately wanted to believe in something.

The next speaker was less inspirational, and you could see why. He was a bureaucrat who was there to make the trains run on time.

I don't remember his name. He was short, squat, had a squeaky voice, and reminded me of a vole. He told us that, first and foremost, we were not currently employees of the Central Intelligence Agency. We had been asked to apply and they would decide who would be accepted. We would be given packets when we left that day explaining when and where to report for the screening sessions.

He finished up by explaining that we could tell *no one* that we were being considered by the CIA for employment. He was very clear and said it was illegal for us to do so. He educated us on several potential fake answers we could give to family and friends who asked.

Somewhere — buried deep in my self-absorbed psyche — there was something disquieting about the juxtaposition of the rousing patriotic call to action followed immediately with a detailed instructional on lying to your mom, dad and girlfriend.

CHAPTER 9

The next day I reported to a building farther down Constitution Avenue near the Lincoln Memorial that turned out to be one of the early CIA buildings. There were several folks already there, even though I was early. We sat in a rather beat-up room without windows and waited as others checked in.

Several of the guys were smoking, and the room seemed dense with bad air and gray exhaled smoke that hung in stratified layers.

Finally, the group — about thirty all told — were invited into an adjacent room with old-fashioned school desks arrayed around a chalkboard. I grabbed a desk up front and tried to appear confident and focused. I was nervous about how they intended to "screen" applicants.

A man named Mr. Munroe walked to the front and explained that we were about to spend the next five days undergoing a series of evaluations. He warned us not to talk to anyone — especially our fellow candidates — about the details of the tests. Munroe was particularly concerned about the lie-detector tests and said it would be a breach of security to reveal anything about the procedure.

And he emphasized again that each of us was to adopt a plausible "cover story" for why we were in Washington and to use it "around the clock."

The psychological tests were interesting but predictable. I took a calculated guess that they were looking for obedient foot soldiers in the war on communism. They told us not to "slant" our responses, but I didn't really care. In retrospect, I'm not sure if I was being reckless because I was supremely confident in outguessing them, or whether I was being self-destructive out of ambivalence about joining the agency.

We showed up each day at the same building off Constitution Avenue and I began to notice that our class was shrinking in size. I guessed that some candidates were being washed out. The knowledge of this made me both confident about getting this far, but also nervous that I was going to be shown the door next.

As our group was whittled down, the survivors grew familiar with each other. I became friendly with a guy named Chuck Nealon. He was a big guy who walked around with an infectious grin and seemed so damn happy. He also broke wind whenever Munroe left the room, no matter the ribbing or threats he received from the other survivors. I remember feeling awed in Chuck's presence; how could a man feel so confident in life that he could smile and fart all day without a care in the world?

On Friday it was my turn to take the lie detector test. They warned us they would ask anything — "aaannyything," Munroe said. It unnerved me to think that they would delve into my family or sex life, to the extent that I had a sex life.

I was led into a room and hooked up to the machine. A bald fellow in his late thirties was the technician and he looked exhausted. He had me fill out a brief questionnaire and then warned me not to try to outsmart the machine. "Answer truthfully and everything would be fine," he said.

He started out asking simple things like my name, address, age, and stuff like that. Then he grew increasingly personal.

"Have you ever stolen something?"

"Uh, yes," I said.

"What did you steal?"

"A comic book."

"Who did you steal the comic book from?"

"The corner drug store. Do you need to know which one?" I asked.

"No — just answer my questions, please."

"OK."

"Have you ever stolen money?"

"No."

And these went on for a while until he shifted to sex.

"Have you ever had sex with a woman?"

"Um, unfortunately, no."

"Just 'no' is fine."

"Have you ever masturbated?"

"Um, yes."

"Do you masturbate more than once a week?"

"Depends."

"Just yes or no."

"Yes, I guess sometimes."

"Just 'yes' or 'no.'"

"Um, 'yes,' I guess."

"Have you ever masturbated in the presence of another man?"

"No!"

"Have you ever kissed a man on the lips?"

"No."

"Have you ever had sex with a man?"

"No."

"Have you ever wanted to have sex with a man?"

"No."

These embarrassing questions trailed off; then he delved into my relationships with foreign nationals for too long and in painstaking detail. I answered "No" to virtually all of these questions.

Then it was over, and I was allowed to leave.

Later that afternoon I was told to report to a room in the basement.

I knocked and entered. Sitting behind a gray metal desk was Mr. Munroe. He gestured for me to sit in the only other chair in the small room. The look on his face was blank, and I feared this was my "kiss-off" exit interview; another washed-up CIA candidate who didn't make the grade.

And in truth, I was still ambivalent about joining the agency. On the one hand, it did seem like exciting work, and the cause of fighting communism anywhere in the world seemed about as important as one could imagine. But my heart wasn't really in it — was anyone's? — and I had difficulty feeling a real passion for this kind of work.

"Mr. Haliday, I want to thank you for joining us this week," he said with barely a flicker of interest. "The results of your evaluations suggest you will be an outstanding new employee of the Central Intelligence Agency."

The fact that he never smiled, nor suggested he was doing anything more than reading a list of things to buy at the supermarket, seemed odd.

He did, though, extend his right hand as he stood. He finished up his dispirited congratulation by offering me another envelope.

"This letter will tell you where to report to next. And please, Haliday, remember your cover. You are now an employee of the agency and are bound by rules of secrecy that have serious penalties if breached. Is that clear?"

"Yes, sir."

"Excellent. You may leave the building now after signing out, and we will see you Monday morning. Good day."

"Thank you, sir," I said.

Walking out of the office and up the long flight of stairs to the sign-out room, I felt the glow of accomplishment and the self-important smugness that comes with winning where others have failed.

And I began to worry about telling my father about my career choice. Should I send him a letter? Call him long distance? Wait until he visited Washington again? I knew he was not going to be happy, but I also thought he might come around when he heard that his son passed muster in a hyper competitive group.

The phone rang at 10:30 that night at the townhouse. I thought it was one of my friends calling about hitting a couple of bars on M Street, but it was my father's secretary Christine in Washington. Even when he was overseas, he always kept a secretary at headquarters.

"Is this Nick?" she said.

"Yes, it is. Who's this?"

"It's Christine from your father's office in Washington."

"Oh, hi."

"Listen, Nick, your father is on his way back to the states on an unannounced visit. He wanted me to call you to make sure you knew he was coming and were available to see him on Sunday."

"This Sunday?"

"Yes. As I said, he's already in the air and will be home on Sunday morning. Are you going to be there?"

"Uh, sure, Christine. I should be here. Is something wrong with my father?"

"Not that I know of," she said.

"OK. Well, thanks for the call."

"Sure, Nick. Take care now."

After hanging up I went to the kitchen and took a can of Schlitz out of the fridge. Preoccupied with the call, I slowly searched and found the can opener. I painstakingly popped a triangle-shaped cut in the top of the can, rotated it, and popped the other side.

Taking a very long sip, I nervously wiped the thin froth mustache and took another long drink.

I was eating toast and drinking a cup of coffee when I heard the lock on the front door being turned.

There were some muffled voices as I recognized my father.

"No, that's OK. I have it. No need to bring it in. Thank you. Have a nice day."

I heard him trudging up the stairs.

"Hello?" I said. "Father?"

He grunted and I heard him sigh in what seemed like exhaustion.

He walked into the living room, took off his coat, and dropped it on the couch. I heard him walk into the kitchen and looked up to see that he was still dressed in a suit, though his tie was loosened, and his top button was undone.

"Any more coffee?" he asked.

"Sure." I got up, pulled a mug from the cupboard and poured him a cup.

He shuffled over to join me at the small kitchen table. His eyes were bloodshot, and he looked worn out and preoccupied. In those days it took forever to fly Pan American World Airlines across the Pacific in propeller-powered planes.

He looked into his coffee pensively as if it were some kind of wishing well.

"Nick," he said, still looking at the coffee. "What are you doing?" It was more pleading than a request.

"I'm not sure I know what you mean, Father."

"You know what I mean," he cut me off. "Did you think I was not going to find out? Didn't you think that someone at the agency would have noticed your father is a high-ranking official at the State Department? I assume they told you that you needed a security clearance?"

"Oh, that," I said, now looking down at my coffee. "I guess I was going to tell you the next time you came home. Or in a letter. I'm not sure."

I know how I imagined telling my father because I had rehearsed it several times in my head, but this was not unfolding as planned.

"Nick, I've thought a lot about us since I found out. The three of us, including your mother. I guess I keep waiting for you to get over what is bothering you, but it never seems to happen. I have a feeling you're still trying to punish me, to hurt me in some way. Is that true?"

"No," I said. "What makes you think that?"

"Nick, let's not kid around. This is serious stuff. You are now an employee of an organization I despise; no, not 'despise,' more like 'hate' with every molecule in my body. And you know that. On the long flight over I kept trying to figure out why you never told me you were interested in the agency. And then I remembered that brief conversation we had about you joining the Foreign Service. In retrospect, I think you were toying with me, Nick."

"I don't think so," I said. I had trouble looking him in the eye so I kept rotating my coffee mug, a quarter-turn every few seconds, like a clock winding down.

"No, Nick. I'm convinced you were toying with me. And I realize now — I admit to being naïve about some things — that you hate me." At this he paused and I could feel him choking. It's funny, but all the years since my mother's death we had never hashed it out like this.

"I guess you still won't forgive me for your mother's death," he said. "But, to be honest, Nick — and perhaps you'll see this one day — I don't need to be forgiven. I didn't kill your mother. Your mother killed your mother. Perhaps, just perhaps, you cannot stand the thought of being angry at your mother for putting you and me through this agony. So, it's easier for you to hate me."

My heart was beating so loud and with such force that I thought it was going to rip out of my rib cage. I thought he was going to cry but he didn't.

"Now, Nick, I'll only ask once, because it seems that you have your mind set on this, but is there anything that I can do — anything under the sun — to get you to change your mind about joining the agency?"

I replied so quickly that it shocked me as much as it did him: "No."

He sighed slightly, pushed his coffee away and stood up. "I'm going to take a nap now and will be leaving tomorrow to return to Tokyo. If I don't see you before I leave, good luck in your new endeavor."

"Thanks," I said.

"And, Nick?"

"Yes?"

"I want you to remember what I'm telling you now. Are you listening?"

"Yes."

"Here goes: Don't believe a goddamn thing the agency tells you. If you assume they're lying to you each step of the way, then you'll come out in one piece. Otherwise," he shook his head, "you're cooked."

"OK. Thanks."

He trudged upstairs to his bedroom and I remained in the kitchen staring at my coffee.

I was stunned that he confronted me directly with my mother's death. Was he right? Was it easier to blame him than my mother? My perfectly constructed narrative about a family destroyed by the State Department and an absent workaholic father started to crumble.

I hated her drinking. I hated being embarrassed by her. I hated being the sober "adult" in the house when he was gone. So why was I protecting her cherished memory?

Like my father, I drank my coffee black. I stared down at the smooth, ebony surface and saw my reflection. I didn't like what I saw.

CHAPTER 10

Camp Peary sits on ten thousand acres of scrubland and forest on the James River next to Williamsburg, Virginia. It originally belonged to the Navy but was handed over to the agency after WWII and became its training facility for spies.

I was sent there as part of the so-called Class of 1957. More importantly, it meant I was being trained to go into the field under the Directorate of Plans, but later its name changed to the Directorate of Operations. Sitting behind a desk fighting communists with a pencil and a telephone — which was the Directorate of Intelligence — seemed boring.

They put us through a mini-boot camp at Peary, even dressing us in Army fatigues. My newfound friend Chuck was also assigned to Peary.

We reported in August and it was ungodly hot and humid. Most of the guys in training — there were forty of us — were athletic and fairly fit. I was out of shape, so it was rough for me in the beginning.

But like an overgrown Boy Scout I found myself absorbed by the fine art of spying: how to secretly open and reseal an envelope, how to tail a suspect through city streets, how to use a live drop or a dead drop for moving messages, how to use code, how to use ciphers.

And they trained us in the more dangerous pursuits: how to kill another human being quickly from behind, how to use common household ingredients to poison someone, how to stab someone to kill them in one stroke, how and where to shoot someone to kill them instantly at short range.

To me these things were nothing more than higher-level Boy Scout merit badges; a scout got a badge for building a crystal radio set, and another one for signaling with Morse Code. Now I was getting one for surreptitiously tailing a spy and another one for killing him with a single shot in the back of the head. It was the Boy Scout continuum, simple as that.

Our group of male trainees broke into two camps: the snotty, smart-alecky, know-nothing college graduates, and the grizzled, steely-eyed military veterans. It never occurred to me that military veterans would want to join the CIA, but sure enough, there were plenty — about one-third of the Class of 1957. And many of them had fought in Korea. There were two Marines who had been caught in the disaster at the Chosin Reservoir, and by the look of them during boot camp, they had probably killed more people than I knew.

When the vets fired their weapons during training, whether it was an M1 rifle, a .38-caliber Smith & Wesson, or a snazzy little P28 East German submachine gun, they braced themselves appropriately and fired confidently.

My first experience with the old M1 rifle was embarrassing. First, it was much heavier than I imagined at nearly ten pounds. Second, shooting in the prone position with the rifle webbing wrapped around your elbow was very uncomfortable. And lastly, well, the kick from the .30-caliber round was more than I expected.

Sgt. Ferry, our instructor, walked us through the rifle's operation and then took us out to the range. When my group took their turn at target practice, I couldn't get my eye situated properly behind the sight. I was still trying to get it just right when Ferry came up behind me.

"Jesus Christ, Haliday, what are you waiting for, the goddamn

Chinese Army to introduce themselves to you personally? Fire the damn thing!"

And of course, I did. But the recoil jammed the rifle butt onto my chin with such force that it cut the inside of my cheek. And then I made the one mistake you don't make on a rifle range training to be an American spy.

I said, "Ouch."

I thought I was saying it to myself, but Ferry heard it.

"What did you say, Haliday?" he yelled.

"Nothing, sir."

"I heard you say something. Sounded an awful lot like something a sissy would say."

"Not me, sir."

"You sure, Haliday?"

"Positive."

"Positive 'what'?"

"Positive, sir."

My friend Chuck was a practical joker and it didn't take him long to dislike the group of vets. Whereas most of us college kids were self-con-scious and reticent around the vets, Chuck took the opposite approach. He disliked their snobbism, I guess you'd call it, and took on the vets with his practical jokes.

There was at least one joke that stands out in my memory, though not because it was particularly funny. Of all things, it involved salt and pepper shakers.

Camp Peary had a mess hall like any other boot camp, although it was more relaxed, I would guess. There was a food line at the front where guys would wait in line single file for their glop. After being served you'd go sit with your friends at one of many long tables.

A group of us college guys might be sitting on both sides of a long table, but twenty feet away would be a group of vets sitting at the same table. Every five feet or so there would be a set of a standard all-American salt and peppers shakers with thick glass barrels and stainless-steel tops. One morning a group of us were late to breakfast and most of the seats were taken. We grabbed our glop and sat down at one of the few open spaces left.

But behind us in the food line came three vets, one of them a particularly rough guy named Victor Kolchenko.

Victor was a first-generation Russian from the Chicago area and had fought in Korea. He was a huge guy, well-proportioned, with an impeccable flat-top haircut and steely blue eyes. Victor made no mystery of his dislike for us college kids. He thought we were idiots and would mutter things under his breath — which we could all hear — during the field exercises. Things like "Look at those fucking pansies," or "They let homos in now, do they?"

Well, this one morning our group had snagged the last table although there was a spot at the end that was open. Don't ask me how Chuck even noticed the set of circumstances involving Victor. Like the other guys in our group, I was only interested in chowing down on the pretend food they gave us. But Chuck noticed that Victor would be sitting next to us in a few minutes.

"Hey, Haliday," he said to me. "Give me those salt and pepper shakers down there."

"Huh?" I said looking up from my plate of glop.

"Give me those shakers. Quick, before Victor sits down."

I slid down the bench, grabbed the two shakers and slapped them in front of Chuck.

We watched Chuck perform a nefarious trick I've never seen anyone else do since. He unscrewed the caps off the shakers and set them down. Taking his paper napkin, he tore off a piece the size of a dollar bill and put it over the open top of the saltshaker. Using his forefinger, he gently poked down the napkin over the barrel of the saltshaker creating a tiny pocket perhaps a quarter inch deep.

Without looking up, Chuck said, "Where's Victor?"

"Laughing with one of the cooks," said the guy next to me.

"Whatever you're doing, Chuck, you better hurry," I said.

Chuck next grabbed the peppershaker and commenced to pour pepper into the small pocket he created into the top of the saltshaker. Then he took the stainless-steel salt top and screwed it gingerly onto the base over the thin paper napkin. When he was finished, the saltshaker looked normal except the spare napkin stuck out all around the top.

Chuck tore off all those dangling pieces of napkin. It finally occurred to me what he was doing and I laughed out loud. He had created a tiny pocket of pepper cupped underneath the top of the saltshaker. The pocket was so shallow that there was no way to see it through the glass.

"Shhhh!" he said, screwing the peppershaker top on quickly.

Finishing up, he pushed them over to me and said "Put 'em back. Hurry."

I slid down and deposited the shakers at the end of the table and quickly joined the group.

Sure enough, Victor and two of his buddies sat down at the end of our table and ignored us as they usually did. I tried not to be obvious, but I couldn't resist straining my peripheral vision looking at them.

The food was so awful we normally covered it with copious amounts of salt and pepper and my eyes lit up when Victor grabbed the shakers and absently covered his food with salt and pepper, only he was really covering his food with pepper and more pepper.

Then his two buddies did the same thing while exchanging a joke and laughing raucously.

Victor started eating his glop and…nothing happened. He and his pals just kept chatting and eating.

I turned to Chuck. "Well, that was really exciting. Thanks for the entertainment."

"Just wait," Chuck said. "You'll see."

And sure enough, after a few bites, Victor stopped and reached over for the saltshaker. This time he really shook the salt out of the shaker onto his food — only, of course, it was just more pepper.

Putting it down, he took his fork and stabbed a humongous pile of what they called scrambled eggs and jammed it into his mouth without looking.

"Chuck, you are a diabolical genius," said the guy next to me under his breath.

Victor suddenly grimaced, as if he had been stung by a bee, and looked down at this plate. It had to have been covered in pepper. He quickly grabbed his thick white ceramic mug of coffee and washed down the eggs.

Now, Victor and his buddies looked at their food, then the shakers. Victor grabbed the saltshaker with his huge paw of a right hand and held it up to his face. Then he shook it a couple of times into his left palm to inspect it in the dim light of the cafeteria.

"What the hell!" I heard him say.

At that point, our little group burst out laughing, and Victor snapped his head and glared at us.

"He's going to kill you," I said to Chuck, trying not to laugh.

"Why would he kill me?" Chuck said laughing. "You were the last guy to touch the shakers."

The Russian stood up and came down to the table and stood over us, all six feet and two inches of him.

"What did you assholes do?" he demanded.

"What are you talking about?" Chuck said. "Did what?"

"You know," he said. "Someone messed up my food."

"How did they mess up your food?" Chuck said.

It occurred to me that Victor had no idea where the extra pepper came from since he hadn't deconstructed the faulty saltshaker yet.

"I don't know but it's messed up. One of you assholes did it, and I know it. I won't forget it."

"Sure, Victor," Chuck said, finishing his coffee and standing up.

We all stood up with Chuck, not wanting to be within a square mile of Victor when he unscrewed the saltshaker top.

A week later Victor and I were on the same four-man team doing a training surveillance tail on one of the instructors through the streets of downtown Norfolk. It was a classic diamond configuration, and I was on the bottom "point" of the diamond; Victor was on the opposite side of the street, another guy was slightly ahead of our subject, and Chuck was running point.

Victor was supposed to stop and take off his hat if our subject did anything unusual like duck into a retail store, at which point I was supposed to hole up and window shop — anything to keep a safe distance as the last point on the diamond.

I watched Victor stop in front of a newspaper vending machine, put in a coin, then take off his hat and wipe his brow. I stopped and began window shopping at Murphy's Department Store. I tried to keep sight of Victor across the street in the reflection of the plate glass, but it was difficult when people walked by and obstructed my view.

Finally, I turned and looked directly at Victor, but he was gone. Panicked, I looked up my side of the street for our subject and couldn't see him or Victor's opposite number. Then I started up the street. I couldn't find anyone — our subject, Victor, or his opposite number. I finally skidded into Chuck, who looked just as lost.

"Where is everyone?" I hissed.

"Beats me!" he said trying to sound nonchalant.

"Victor took off his hat; so I treaded water. Now what!"

I turned around, scanning the other side of the street, and my heart fluttered a bit when I saw the instructor standing next to Victor and the other guy, shaking his head in disgust.

"Dammit," I said. "Chuck, we're screwed."

At the de-brief, the instructor was all over me.

"Sir, I saw Victor take off his hat, so I held steady like I'm supposed to. Then he disappeared when I turned around."

"I never took off my hat," Victor said. "That's crap, sir."

"I didn't see him take off his hat," said the other guy.

Chuck, looking conflicted, said, "Well, I was too far away to see what happened."

"Haliday, you pull that shit again, and you might be on the next train out of here," the instructor said.

"Sir," I said pleading, "he took off his hat in front of the newspaper rack."

"You guys get out of here," he said.

On the way down the stairs Victor said in a high-pitched mocking tone, "He took off his hat, he took off his hat. You homos."

That night, before Chuck got into his bunk, I emptied an entire saltshaker onto his bottom sheet. For good measure, I put the empty shaker under his pillow.

CHAPTER 11

Toward the end of training two men began to observe us. We had never seen them before. They stood off to the side of the field exercises, or at the back of the classroom. We noticed they would sometimes huddle with the instructors.

It made us nervous because, to our great surprise, not everyone in the class of 1957 matriculated to spydom.

By the third week of training, they had already sent three guys home: two college kids and one vet. The scuttlebutt was the vet was sent back because he was "unstable." We were never sure why the two kids were discharged. Chuck said they had bad breath.

While I entered the spy business for no particular reason other than it seemed exciting and it might irritate my father, I was competitive enough to *not* want to fail.

The longer the two new observers hung around, the more troubled we became. Chuck didn't seem to care. "Who gives a crap?" was his favorite line. But the rest of us college kids were driving ourselves crazy with theories on these two new observers. One of my friends named them, "Tom & Jerry, the Looney Tunes."

And just like that, Tom & Jerry vanished, and we went on with our training, confident that we passed muster.

I wrote to my father sparingly while in training and spoke to him on the phone twice. I'll admit that I was envious of the other guys who would call their parents or girlfriends and talk forever. Of course, we couldn't talk about our training — the official cover was we were at a seminar on governmental relations.

Still, I wished I could talk to someone in my family. Loneliness began to creep in, and it occurred to me that I might be depressed. I had no mother; I wasn't close to my father, and I had no siblings. I was not close to any of my cousins, uncles or aunts.

Several times I thought of calling my father, but a gnawing stubbornness surfaced, as it usually did, and I simply let it pass.

My substitute for a family were memories of my mother. The *good* ones, of course: her chatting with me around the kitchen table and smoking up a storm, tossing her head back to make a point and blowing the smoke out of the corner of her mouth, or dressing me for school in Hong Kong, licking her thumb absently and then pushing down an errant tuft of hair on my little head. Those were happy memories and I kept them right in front of me to push out the loneliness.

I wondered how she would feel about me becoming a spy. My guess is she would have approved, as long as I was trying to get ahead, that is, to be the chief spy.

About a week before our training ended, I was asked to report to one of the small administrative buildings at Peary. This was unusual, and when the runner had delivered the message, a couple of guys ribbed me pretty good.

"Haliday, you've done it now. They found out about your Communist Party affiliations."

Another one said, "Just remember, I told you *not* to talk about Eisenhower that way. He's our president, you know."

Yuk, yuk.

When I entered the building there was no receptionist, just a couple of rooms with doors closed. One of them was open and had a light on. I heard voices.

"Hello?" I said.

"Oh, yes. Haliday. Come in."

I almost fainted when I saw who was in the room. It was Tom & Jerry. Just the two of them, no one else from the training program.

"Hi," said the tall one, standing up and shaking my hand with a big smile. "I'm Joe Elia. This is Gardner Morse. We're from headquarters."

We shook hands, and I just stood there, not knowing whether I was getting my cut slip or ordered back for more training.

"Sit down," Elia said, gesturing to a chair.

I tried to remain calm and feigned a smile.

"Haliday," he said, "my partner and I have been scouting out your class of recruits."

"Yes, we noticed," I said, the cocky Haliday emerging while under duress.

"Ha," Elia said smiling at his partner. "I guess we're hard to miss."

"Well, anyway, we've been searching for a candidate for a special project. We originally looked within the current crop of agents for our guy, but they really didn't fit the profile."

I was confused and had trouble understanding him. It almost seemed like they were flattering me.

"We need someone who is young," Elia said.

"And professorial," Morse said, speaking for the first time.

"Young and professorial," Elia said.

There was silence in the room. It finally dawned on me that I was the person they'd chosen — the "young and professorial" guy, whatever the hell that meant.

"We think you might be our guy," Elia said.

"Well, thanks," I said uncertainly. I had no idea what they were talking about, of course, but I also felt a rush of pride at being *the chosen one.*

"We've talked to your instructors," Morse said, "and they believe you can do the job."

"Well," I said smiling, "thanks for the vote of confidence. Just what is this project that you need help on?"

"Ah, yes, the project," Elia said, sitting back in his chair. "It's an extremely important effort that has great urgency within the agency. That's why we've been searching for just the right fellow."

"OK," I said, waiting.

"Do you know much about English Literature?" Morse asked.

I didn't answer right away because for a moment I wondered if I was hallucinating. English Literature? Wasn't I being trained as a field agent in the clandestine services of our government?

"Um, in what sense do you mean?" I answered. "Have I ever read any? Yes, of course."

"Do you think you could teach it?" he said.

"Teach it?" I asked, sitting forward with a jolt. "To whom?"

"To college kids."

"Jeeze, I don't know. I'm not really training here as a teacher." What the hell did they need a college English Lit teacher for?

"Do you think you could pass as an English Lit teacher to Central American college students," Elia said.

"Huh?" was all I could muster.

"To Panamanian college students to be exact," Morse said.

"Well, you got me there. I'm not really sure what to say."

Tom & Jerry exchanged glances and then turned to face me.

"Haliday — Nick," Morse corrected himself, "we're looking for an agent to go undercover at the University of Panama. As an English Lit teacher. We would normally never approach someone just coming out of Peary with such an important mission, but we just can't find the right person. You look like our guy."

"Please don't misunderstand me," I said. "I appreciate your confidence in me. It's just that I think I can do more than teach Chaucer for the CIA."

Once again, they exchanged glances, but this time I noticed that Elia emitted a sigh of frustration.

He stood up from the edge of a gray metal desk. "Do you know what happened last year in Egypt at the Suez Canal?"

"Well, um, let me think. Wasn't there some military action? Was Britain involved?"

"Very good," he said. "Last year that bastard President Nasser in Egypt suddenly decided that even though Britain and France had built the Suez Canal, and were operating it under a *legal* lease, that he would just take it over. So, he nationalized the Suez Canal."

"Just stole it," Morse said.

"Out and out robbery," Elia said. "Britain, France — with help from our friends the Israelis — sent military forces there to get it back."

"It was theirs rightfully," Morse said.

"But that bastard Nasser," Elia said, "he turns to the Soviet Union for help."

"Help!" Morse said, waving his hand as if in distress. "Help."

"And sure enough the Soviets threaten to send troops to support the Egyptians. All shit breaks out. So our State Department" — at this, they roll their eyes in derision — "convinces Eisenhower to back off and give the stupid canal to the Egyptians. 'It's not worth World War III,' they say."

"They don't even know how to operate a canal," Morse says. "They still ride camels, for god's sake."

I'm following the current affairs class by Tom & Jerry and am modestly intrigued, but the room falls silent again as the two agents stare at me. I'm not sure what to say, so I just stare back. I notice a fly orbiting the single light bulb on the ceiling. Stupidly, incessantly, the insect keeps throwing itself against the thin glass shell of the bulb, making little pinging sounds.

"Nick," Elia said. "Do you see where we're going with this?"

"I have absolutely no idea where you're going."

"We have a canal too," he said.

"Of course," I said.

"It's in Panama," he said. "It is the largest public works project in our history."

"The French couldn't build it," Morse said. "They tried and failed miserably."

"We have a ninety-nine-year lease on the canal," Elia said. "It's a vital part of our national security. It allows us to move ships and vast amounts of material to hotspots on either side of the globe."

"We can't lose the canal," Morse said. "Can't happen."

Finally — painfully — catching up to Tom & Jerry, I said, "Are we in danger of losing the Panama Canal?"

"Not if we can help it," Morse said with John Wayne-like swagger.

"Nick, the Soviets are starting brushfires for us everywhere in the world and they would like nothing better than to have our canal nationalized," Elia said. "Every time we turn around they're starting another fire. We had to get really nasty with that Guatemalan President Arbenz a couple of years back."

"That was a real mess," Morse said. "But we sent that commie packing."

"And now, believe it or not, even though the Panamanian government is our good friend, there's a fire there that's getting out of hand. A group of leftists is agitating for the Americans to go home and turn over the canal."

"We built the damn thing with our sweat and blood," Morse said. "And they just expect us to walk away. Not gonna happen."

"Nick, the opposition seems to be centered at the university there," Elia said. "The students seem really agitated and are undoubtedly being encouraged and funded by the Soviets. There have been several demonstrations. The last one was much bigger than we anticipated.

The government there cannot seem to get it under control. And it's delicate for them because the agitators are raising the flag of nationalism. We can't wait any longer for the Panamanian government to clean it up. This thing is picking up steam."

"But English Literature? Help me with that one."

"There is a rotating professorship at the University of Panama," Elia said. "It's an English Lit class that's always taught by an American. The unpatriotic bastard there right now will not cooperate with us. His term's up and he'll be replaced with another professor."

"That's you, Nick," Morse said grinning. "Professor Nick Haliday."

"I hate to break it to you guys, but I don't speak Spanish. I'm sure that's in my file."

Smiling, Elia said, "Not to worry, Nick. It's taught in English."

"What am I supposed to do? What would my mission be? Teach Macbeth? 'Out damn spot,'" I said with a smirk.

"What spot?" Morse asked, brow furrowing.

"It was a joke. Nothing," I said.

"Your mission is simple," Elia said. "You help us identify the student leaders. If you penetrate the group effectively, it would be a huge windfall. We could then identify their communist handlers."

"But won't they be awfully suspicious of an American professor?"

"Not if he's a beatnik professor, who writes poetry, listens to rock and roll, and has marched to help the Negro in America."

"Leftist things like that," Morse said. "Anti-American leanings."

"What do you think, Nick?" Elia said. "This sound like something you could do? You up for this? We really need your help. The agency — hell, the president — needs your help!"

"What do you say?" Morse chimed in.

I glanced at the fly, and he was still going at it, throwing himself futilely against the thing that would incinerate him.

"Would I really have to write my own poetry?" I said.

"No, Nick," Elia said smiling. "We have people who do that."

CHAPTER 12

The entire class of 1957 was dispatched back to Washington after a brief graduation ceremony in December. Everyone except me, that is.

I was ordered to undergo a crash-training program to sharpen my rookie skills. I wished Chuck and the others good luck, and I could tell they were envious of the special attention I was getting. Even Victor patted me on the shoulder and said, "Good luck Haliday, you lucky bastard. Stay safe."

I spent a lonely Christmas and New Year's with a handful of Slav recruits at Camp Peary. Many could barely speak English, but apparently, they spoke vodka quite well. For some reason, known only to the folks at Camp Peary, this group was allowed to keep vodka in their rooms and drink after hours to their hearts' content.

On Christmas day I called my father and we chatted for a while about nothing in particular. He kept pressing me on my training, but I said I really couldn't talk about it. Still, it was nice talking to him. He made me feel happy. We both missed my mother, of course, or at least the good and sober mother.

On New Year's Eve, the Slavs put on a crazy party involving vodka, singing, more vodka, and more singing. Everyone was severely hung over the next day; I skulked around holding my head and lamenting my exuberance at solidarity.

I was anxious to get on with my training.

Up to this point, I had only the vaguest idea of what an undercover operation entailed. Personal safety was certainly a theoretical concern, but after the good wishes from Victor — a man who had seen ferocious action against the Chinese in the frozen hills of Korea — I began to worry.

They moved me from the big dorm to a smaller facility where I had a private, though Spartan, room. I was introduced to a new instructor named Seymour. A tall, graceful man with permanent furrows of worry ploughed across his forehead, Seymour walked me through all the clandestine communications channels I was to use in Panama.

For normal, non-emergency communications I was to move a flowerpot from the right corner of my patio to the left corner, and then follow up within twelve hours with a dead drop.

The drop site was to be the last stall toilet in the men's room in the student center at the University of Panama. After closing the stall and preferably urinating — "Get a good stream going if you can," Seymour said straight faced — I was to flush the toilet and quickly slide an envelope between the wall and the porcelain chamber holding water.

"For god's sake, Haliday, make sure that no part of the envelope is sticking out," he said. "We're not bothering to use coded communications on your project. It's too complicated. You get that?"

"I sure do," I said. "Tell me, though, what if I don't have a patio on my apartment in Panama City? What do I do?"

Frowning, Seymour said, "You have a patio, Haliday."

"I do?"

"Of course, why would we be going through this?"

"But no one's told me about my living arrangements. And yet you already know I have an apartment with a patio."

"A second-floor patio," Seymour said.

"OK, a second-floor patio," I continued. "When do I find out all these details?"

"You're finding them out right now and over the next week," he said. "Take plenty of notes and reread your notes. You're going in undercover and you have to be as natural with your new life as possible. Otherwise, you'll be blown. And that can be messy. So, pay attention."

The rest of that day, my trusty notepad in hand, we went over the normal and emergency communications; who my handler was going to be, what kind of information they were interested in getting from me, how to write it up succinctly, and so on.

Now that the training was getting more intense, I was kept segregated from the Slavs and their vodka. I grew lonely. The excitement of the upcoming mission initially made me giddy, but I had no one to share it with. Practically speaking, I was prohibited from sharing the mission anyway, but I still needed human contact.

It occurred to me, rather too late in the game, that the life of a field agent was one of psychological isolation, subterfuge, lying, and manipulation. Sitting alone in my room, I wondered if that was a good choice for me, a guy who even at the unripe age of twenty-three, had already led a life that felt isolated.

That night I dreamed of my father. In the dream he was pushing me back and forth on a swing, standing behind me. I kept trying to engage him in conversation, but he would just smile and push. This odd little dream seemed to go on forever — me swinging back and forth, and my father standing behind me smiling and pushing. Nothing came out of his mouth, not a peep, though it seemed like he wanted to say something.

It must have been a premonition of sorts.

The next morning I was expected to report to Building 19 at 8 a.m. I had just finished brushing my teeth when I heard footsteps and voices in the hallway, followed by a sharp knock on my door.

In popped Tom & Jerry. They looked worried.

"Hey," I said.

"We hate to tell you this," Morse said, "but the mission's been cancelled. Shut down before it started. Thank god it was killed before you were dropped in."

Elia could barely maintain eye contact with me, and his little pal kept shaking his head back and forth in an overly dramatic manner.

"Wait a minute," I said. "What's been cancelled?"

"Your mission," Morse said.

"Why?"

"We don't know any of the details," Elia joined in. "We just know it's been eighty-sixed" — the quaint phrase meaning dead as a doornail.

In a strange vision of clarity, the reason became obvious. The Haliday trait of an aggressive defense surfaced in full force.

"I know what happened," I said standing up. "You finally read my file. You saw who my father is. I bet someone at headquarters said, 'We can't send the only child of Phillip Haliday into this hot zone. If anything happens to him, we've got a lot of explaining to do.'"

They shot each other sharp glances. Bingo.

"Don't be silly," Elia said.

"Missions close all the time for a million reasons," Morse said. "Don't read too much into this."

"Well, I guarantee you one thing," I said defiantly. "I'm calling my father as soon as possible and telling him what happened. He'll be really, really pissed. He's proud that I chose the agency for a career, and he will raise a huge stink about prejudicial treatment for his son. You two better hold on to your hats, because there's going to be hell to pay."

Sometimes when I explode like this, I have no idea who is talking or where the words come from; they just materialize out of nowhere.

"Now wait a minute, Nick," Morse said. "Don't get in an uproar about this. You'll be making a big mistake for such a young employee of the agency. You've got a long career ahead of you here. Don't be bringing in your father."

"Yeah," Elia said.

"Sorry, guys," I said. "This is not personal. But you know as well as I that I'm telling the truth about why this mission got cancelled. It's not really cancelled; it's just cancelled for *me*."

Morse sighed. "Do yourself a favor, Nick. Don't balls this thing up by involving your father. It has nothing to do with him."

"I don't believe you," I said. "I can't wait to get Pop on the horn." Now, where I came up with 'Pop' is a moon shot, since he's always been "Father" to me. But "Pop" made it sound like we were really tight, which we weren't.

Morse turned and whispered something into Elia's ear, then turned to me and said flatly, "Haliday, you are a real pain in the ass, do you know that?"

"Put me back on the mission," I said. "Simple as that."

Elia sighed and just looked at me for about thirty seconds; Morse absently cleaned one of his fingernails. There was not a single sound in the room. "We'll need to chat with some folks," Elia said, and then they left without saying goodbye.

I wondered whether I had just made a catastrophic mistake.

At 8 a.m. I showed up at Seymour's office, but he wasn't there. Walking across the cold, windswept campus I began to wonder about my attempt to bluff Tom & Jerry into keeping me in the Panama program.

I returned to my bedroom and read a Dashiell Hammett crime novel, then had lunch by myself in the mess hall.

They had a small library building, and I perused the collection for an hour or so, then walked glumly back to my room. The giddy excitement of besting Tom & Jerry with my threat gave way to a more sober and troubling rumination. What if the mission was really cancelled for reasons that had *nothing to do* with my father? What if I had it all wrong, and now was creating a crisis that had probably filtered back to headquarters in Washington. Hell, I thought, maybe they'll even cashier me out of the agency for such a brazen attempt to finagle myself back onto a dead mission.

"Dammit," I thought, squinting in the sunlight as I made my way across the campus. "Why can't I just shut the hell up sometimes?"

Lost in my self-flagellating reverie I heard my name being called.

"Haliday!"

Seymour was yelling from the door of the dormitory.

"Haliday, come here. Need to talk to you."

Plodding over I stopped in front of him. He did not bother to come in but just stood there in the door letting a cold blast in.

"Haliday, I've just been told we're back on. I have no idea what happened, who said what to whom. Could care less, really, though you've got Elia and Morse twisted up in knots. My mission is to get you ready as soon as possible. Since we missed today's lesson, we're going to have to make it up tonight. See you after dinner at 7 p.m. in my office."

"Um, OK. I'll see you then."

If it's possible to be happy and worried at the same time, that was me trekking back to my room: happy that I won, and worried that it might have been the stupidest thing I'd ever done.

Elia visited my room later that afternoon. It was the first time I'd interacted with him alone; Morse and he were always paired.

"I guess you've heard we're back on, Haliday," he said, sitting. "The mission is a go."

"That's great," I said. "I hope I didn't go overboard this morning. It was just that I wanted to do this and was disappointed. I don't really expect to be treated differently from anyone else."

"It's a little too late for that," he said flatly.

"Well, I'm sorry nevertheless."

"Duly noted." After a moment lost in thought, he sat forward as if he was going to share something intimate.

"Can I give you some candid advice?" he said.

"Sure."

"Morse would never say this to you, but I'm not Morse, OK?"

"Sure," I said earnestly, leaning forward for his paternal advice.

"If you ever try that shit again on any project that I'm involved with, I will personally find a private moment to cut your dick off and stuff it down your throat so that while you're bleeding to death, I'll have the pleasure of watching you choke as well. Do you understand me?"

His ferocity forced me to lean back involuntarily. I'll never forget the look on his face — it was a frightening view into a deep, dark, and dangerous cavern.

"Duly noted," I said, the smart-ass Haliday emerging again.

He glared a few moments longer. Then, as if a light switch had been flicked, he took a deep breath and smiled. The chameleon-like change frightened me in a way that I had never been frightened before.

"Good," he said. "You'll do fine. Morse and I are done with our assignment — which was to find an appropriate agent — so you'll be introduced to someone else soon. Best of luck." He turned and left the room. I heard his steps reverberating down the cold, darkened hallway and waited until he left the building.

I sat on my bed and looked at my hands. They were shaking. It took me about twenty minutes, but I was finally able to gather myself and go for a walk. I just didn't want to be in that bedroom again if Elia decided to show up. I grabbed the front of my pants to feel for my equipment. It had shriveled quite a bit.

CHAPTER 13

During the rest of my stay at Camp Peary, I was quizzed relentlessly by Seymour and another trainer named Louis.

Question: Who is Ernesto de la Guardia Jr.?

Answer: The new president of Panama.

Question: Is he a friend of the United States?

Answer: Yes, but he appears unwilling or unable to stem nationalistic agitation. He is suspected of being influenced by communist-backed labor unions.

Question: What role does the National Guard play in Panama?

Answer: It is more important than the presidency since it controls the police force and the army. It has been run by the country's ruling families, most notably the Remon and Arias families.

Question: What did Secretary of State John Foster Dulles say last year that incensed the Panamanians?

Answer: He said he did not fear that the Panama Canal would be nationalized like the Suez Canal because the US possessed "rights of sovereignty" there.

Question: Where is the center of leftist agitation for anti-Americanism in Panama?

Answer: Leftist students at the University of Panama, aided and abetted by their communist handlers.

Question: What is your primary mission in Panama?

Answer: Under cover as a visiting American English Literature teacher, I am to identify the leaders of the student cells as well as their communist handlers.

Question: What's your name and where do you hail from?

Answer: My name is Nicholas Baker and I'm a visiting English professor from the University of Maryland. My friends call me Nick.

Question: Who is your handler in Panama and how will you communicate with him?

Answer: His code name is "Don." I will use a dead drop in the university men's room as my primary; secondary is a loose brick enclosure in the parking garage of my apartment.

Question: How do you request a personal meeting with Don?

Answer: Dead drop message saying: "See you at the Tivoli."

Question: How will Don communicate with you?

Answer: A set of blinds in a fourth-story apartment that sits directly above a dry cleaner one block from my apartment will be pulled all the way up. That's when I check the primary dead drop for an incoming message.

Question: What is the protocol for emergency communication?

Answer: For outbound, I will call 342-1123 and say, "Is this the Balboa Yacht Club?" After they say, "You have the wrong number," I'm to drive immediately to a gravel parking lot that is on the west-bound side of the Fort Amador Causeway. Don will show me where it is." For inbound emergencies, I will receive a single phone call at my apartment that will have no one on the line. The phone will ring again thirty seconds later, and then a third time thirty seconds later. I will then drive immediately to our meeting area on the causeway.

Question: As an undercover agent for the Central Intelligence Agency, do you have diplomatic immunity from the government of Panama?

Answer: Negative; I have no immunity.

Question: If arrested by the Panamanian authorities what are you authorized to say?

Answer: That I am a visiting professor of English Literature and demand to speak to an official from the US Embassy in Panama City. Under no circumstances am I to divulge anything except the details of my cover, no matter how long and under what circumstances I'm held in confinement.

"Do you want to say good-bye to anyone in particular?" Seymour said on my last day in camp. "A girlfriend? Your dad? A relative? You know the drill: no details, just that you're being assigned to a new facility by the government."

Loneliness had been gnawing away at me during my time at Camp Peary; the nights were spent reading or watching TV in a lounge. A new class of trainees had started at the camp, and I could hear them jabbering in their native tongue. I guessed they were East Europeans, perhaps even Hungarian, given the thwarted uprising there less than two years earlier. But I never asked who they were, and Seymour and Louis never volunteered the information.

My isolation was probably a good thing because I was not distracted in my training. And yet, when I was alone, especially during the evenings, I would settle into a glum mood, wistfully conjuring up memories of my once intact family.

"You don't want to call anyone?" Seymour asked again. "Your dad? It'll be awhile before you can make contact again."

"Well, maybe I could make a phone call," I said.

"Get on it then, Haliday," he said. "You're flying the coop soon. Our time is nearly up. It's your show now. You'll do fine," Louis said, patting me gently on the shoulder. "A lot of young guys in the agency would love to be getting a chance at this kind of mission. You're a lucky guy."

"If I'm successful, it'll be because of you two guys," I said, embarrassed by my sudden emotion. "You guys are good."

"Ha," Seymour said. "Don't get all mushy on us. Stick by the protocols and you'll do just fine. Now go and make that phone call. You're running out of time."

I sauntered over to the recreation center and picked an empty phone booth out of a row of empty booths. I shut the folding door, and the fan and light came on overhead. Fiddling with a couple of coins I dialed my father's office, not really aware of whether he was even in the States.

Truth be told, I was feeling scared about taking that flight to Miami and onto Panama. Along with the coursework teaching the clandestine arts, and the dead-drop protocols, and the evasive-driving skills, they had taught me how to kill another human being.

Watching the flimsy human-outline paper targets flutter with each round from my pistol during target practice seemed laughably unrealistic. I could do that all day and not feel an iota of compunction for my target. But what was I going to do in the field when confronted with the real person? Was I going to drill a communist provocateur in the middle of his forehead without thinking? It might not be that simple.

The only time during training that I felt the cold, brutal reality of what I might be getting into was the hour that Louis spent teaching me how to strangle someone with a garrote. He used a mannequin to show how to toss the loop over the victim's head from behind, cross your hands behind the victim's back after looping it, and pull furiously towards the opposite shoulder blades, using your knee as a fulcrum in the middle of the victim's back to pull them off balance.

Louis put a towel around his neck and then asked me to try it on him. At first, it seemed comedic. He stood nonchalantly in front of me with a white terry-cloth towel around his neck biding his time while I launched my attack. I whipped the cord over his head and yanked it tightly, raising my left knee into the small of his back. He fell back solidly onto my knee and tried to reach for my wrists but couldn't stretch that far. And for a perverse moment that left me stunned and melancholy the rest of the day, Louis was absolutely helpless in my grasp as I exerted enough pressure through the towel on his carotids and windpipe to force him to gasp several times.

"Good work," he wheezed, as I helped him unwrap the towel. "You've got great technique. You'll have no trouble taking someone out if it comes to that."

In the fishbowl-like confines of the phone booth, I waited while my father's work number rang. Christine answered the phone. "Mr. Haliday's office, may I help you?"

"Hi, Christine, this is Nick Haliday. I haven't talked to you in a while. How are you doing?"

"Good heavens, Nick. It's so nice to hear from you! Boy will your father be happy to hear from you. Can I put you on hold for just a second, he has someone in his office?"

I waited for less than a minute and heard my father's voice.

"Is that you, Nick?"

"Yes, Father. It's me."

"How are you doing? Is everything OK?" He sounded concerned.

"Everything's fine, thanks. Just fine."

"Are you still in training?"

"Gee, I'm not at liberty to discuss anything like that, I'm afraid. But everything's going fine."

"I see," he said, a tinge of disappointment in his voice. "Are you going to be able to visit soon?"

"I'm afraid not. I'll be traveling for a while for my new job."

"Oh," he said.

"I'm looking forward to it," I said, perhaps not as convincingly as I had hoped. "Should be exciting."

"Mmm," he said. "Travel, huh?"

"Yep, travel."

"When do you think I can see you again? It's been, well, kind of lonely around here."

"Yeah, well it's been kind of the same here," I said. "I'm sorry I wasn't able to get away. They have a rush project that I'm involved in. I'm new to this kind of stuff. Still, I'm looking forward to getting the heck out of here."

"Are you in Peary?" he said.

"I don't think I'm allowed to answer that. Do you know about Camp Peary?"

"I gather it's hot down there in the summer."

I laughed. "That would be an understatement."

"Well, I worry about you. I know you don't want to hear that, but I do. And I miss seeing you."

"Unfortunately, I'll be leaving soon. Wished I could have gotten some time off, but this project is high-priority. Or that's what they're saying. I don't really know when I'll be back in town," I said. "They tell us not to plan too far ahead for anything."

There was a pause on the other side of the line. Then he said simply and wistfully, "Well, I miss you, Nick. I hope you're safe. Please be careful out there."

"I miss you too," I said, and I meant it. "Talk to you when I return."

"Bye," he said. "Be safe."

"Bye," I replied, pushing the stainless-steel handle of the phone down to disconnect the call.

I sat in the booth for several minutes, cut off from the real world by the high-pitched whir of the fan and the soundproofed booth. A self-pitying wave washed over me: why was I so alone? Why did my mother have to die? Why couldn't I get over my discomfort with my father? And how, in god's name, did I end up in this swamp of a camp on the banks of the James River practicing killing people? So I can pretend to be a professor at the University of Panama?

So this is spy craft.

CHAPTER 14

The flight from Miami to Panama City was bumpy and crowded. I had a window seat and a chain-smoking man in his forties had the aisle. An English Lit textbook sat in my lap along with a syllabus used by my predecessor.

Somewhere over the Caribbean, the fellow said, "So what are you studying?"

"Oh, this?" I said. "It's a textbook. I'm an English Lit teacher. This is the book I'll be using."

"An English teacher? Gee, that seems like an interesting job. Where are you going to teach?"

"The University of Panama. I'm on a one-year visiting professorship there. I've never been to Central America — or anywhere outside the United States really — so this is really exciting." The words came tumbling out so naturally and my feigned enthusiasm was so authentic that I smiled. *This can work, I thought. Seymour said my "natural cockiness" made me perfect for this line of work. Maybe he was right.*

He introduced himself as Phil Hardwick, an American businessman whose company owned several fishing fleets throughout Central and South America. He said they had a tuna fleet in Colon, Panama, and that he was there to check up on them.

"You can't believe how corrupt these boat captains are," he said, shaking his head. "They report one-and-a-half tons of bluefin landed, and you pay them the going rate, plus a bonus. But when you send the fish off to be processed, it never equals one-and-a-half tons. Not even close. We can't figure out if they're really landing that amount, or whether on the way to the processor someone dips into the shipment. Or even if the processor is stiffing us."

I asked him how he was going to get to the truth.

"There is no 'truth' per se down there, professor," he said distractedly, taking a long drag on his unfiltered Chesterfield. "Best you can do, in my judgment, is to just get a piece of the truth — not the whole thing, mind you — just a sliver and then call it a victory. At least that's what I tell my boss." He chortled, twisting his mouth, and blew a long stream of blue smoke toward the ceiling of the plane. "Otherwise, you'll drive yourself crazy. I can't figure out if it's the weather, the jungle, the bizarre animals, or the people, but nothing is what it seems."

"Well, thanks for the advice," I said. "Luckily, I'm not dealing with fish, just students, and books. That's all."

Panama City International Airport was small. I was through customs quickly and made my way to the exit to find my guide, a Mr. Delgado, who had been sent by the university to welcome me.

"Mr. Baker?" said a young man walking up to me.

"Yes, I am Mr. Baker. Are you Mr. Delgado?"

"Yes, Señor," he said. "How was your trip?"

"It was great," I said. "I can hardly wait to see the school. This is very exciting," I gushed. "I've never been outside the United States before."

"Ah, well then," he said. "You will like Panama."

In fact, driving out of the airport and through the city's outskirts, there was nothing to like. Mr. Delgado kept up a constant patter about the history of the country while I visually swept the strange surroundings. The airport was east of the city near a collection of shantytowns that sprawled haphazardly. I had been warned that parts of the country were desperately poor, but nothing quite prepared me for this.

Most of the homes were made of a combination of discarded retail signs, cardboard, plywood, and corrugated metal. Brown-skinned children walked around nearly naked, while dogs of nearly every size lay about in the shade. The smell of burning leaves and wood permeated the car.

"There are many poor people," Delgado said. "They come from the countryside to look for work, a better life. You cannot blame them, I suppose. But still, it places burdens on the government and as you can see there are hygienic concerns."

Perhaps it was the heat and humidity that swirled through the open windows, or maybe it was the fatigue from the long flight but sitting in the front seat with Mr. Delgado I was suddenly gripped with a rush of anxiety. I'm not sure what I expected to see in Panama, but the absolute *foreignness* of the surroundings was disorienting. How the hell was I going to operate in this alien culture and landscape?

The self-doubt sat with me in the car like a fog while Delgado pattered on. I managed to nod affirmatively at his comments, but I felt small and isolated in the passenger seat of his Oldsmobile. By the time we reached the middle-class sections of the city, I was feeling more grounded.

We stopped in a small parking garage under a six-story apartment building. He helped me carry one of my suitcases up the stairs — there were no elevators — and unlocked the doors to my apartment. As Seymour predicted, I had a second-story apartment with a patio.

Delgado offered to take me to pick up my long-term rental car, but I begged off, telling him I needed to take a nap. The English Department was planning a reception-cocktail party for me that evening, and I wanted to be rested.

Seymour had warned that most mistakes in undercover operations are caused by fatigue and alcohol: Agents say the stupidest goddamn things when they're exhausted and half-cocked.

"Of course, Mr. Baker," Delgado said. "I will pick you up at 6 o'clock if that is agreeable to you."

"Yes, that would be perfect. And it's Nick, not Mr. Baker."

"Of course, Nick," he said, but I could see he was uncomfortable with that level of informality.

I unpacked and methodically examined the entire apartment. Delgado explained that the apartment was used by visiting professors and household items had accumulated that I was welcome to use. I smiled when I saw the patio — it had two aluminum folding chairs with webbed matting. And there was a twelve-inch terra cotta flower-pot on the right side of the patio. Poking up out of it was a wilted hibiscus. I found a coffee cup in the kitchen and made two trips to hydrate the plant.

Standing on the patio, I leaned over the wrought-iron railing and looked at the ground below. *If they come after you through the front door, Seymour said, you need another exit. Make sure you have scouted a landing area if you need to jump. It will happen so fast that you will only have time to jump. Bushes are great cushions for jumping.*

The reception that evening was embarrassingly lavish, and I met so many people that I quickly gave up trying to remember their names. It was held in the university's main administration building, and I estimated there were about fifty people in attendance. The president, a jocular man named Dr. Ernesto Rodriguez, welcomed me in a brief speech in both Spanish and English.

"We are so very happy to welcome young Dr. Baker to the University of Panama," he said, holding a glass of champagne very high. "He continues a tradition of cooperation and partnership with our academic friends in *los Estados Unidos*. His predecessor was an excellent teacher and contributed to the education of our young students. Welcome, Dr. Baker. Would you like to say a few words?"

I should have known it was coming, but the combined effect of the long plane trip, the fatigue, and anxiety about the reality of my mission dulled my senses. I remember I had just put a cracker with some unknown spread into my mouth when Rodriguez asked me to speak.

The room grew uncomfortably quiet as people shooshed each other to listen to the brilliant new young American fake professor.

"Well," I said, swallowing awkwardly, "I want to thank Dr. Rodriguez and the University for welcoming me in such, um, a gracious manner. I'm proud to continue the tradition of this visiting professorship and hope to, um, make a positive contribution to the education of the university's students. And I guarantee," I said with more emotion than my guests could appreciate, "that I have as much to learn as my students do! Thank you."

There was polite applause and several people afterwards made their way by to wish me the best. As the reception started to wind down, Rodriguez tugged my elbow and said, "Dr. Baker, perhaps you would find time to visit me tomorrow? I would like the opportunity to chat in a more informal setting and answer any questions that you may have. Sometime before noon tomorrow?"

"Certainly, Dr. Rodriguez," I said. "I will stop by your office at eleven tomorrow morning. Thank you again for this wonderful reception. I can hardly wait to start."

That night I lay in my bed trying to sleep, but it was too hot. It was April and the end of the so-called dry season there. I could only guess how humid the rainy season would be. I finally opened a couple of windows and turned on a small oscillating fan that was on the bedroom dresser. The rhythmic whooshing of the fan finally lulled me into a fitful sleep.

Less than a year ago I had been wondering what I wanted to do when I grew up, and here I was a pretending to be an English professor in a Central American country in the service of my country's clandestine services. And if spying and holding a tight cover in place were not my only challenges, I had also to function as an English Lit teacher. I prayed that none of these kids really knew Chaucer from F. Scott Fitzgerald.

CHAPTER 15

I waited in Dr. Rodriguez's outer office for thirty minutes. His secretary, who did not speak English, pointed to a chair and said, *"Por favor, siéntese hasta que el Dr. Rodríguez esté disponible."*

Officially, I understood very little Spanish, but in fact, I was given a crash course from a tutor at Camp Peary. The teacher, a woman in her fifties named Janice Wilcox, led me through simple phrases including greetings like, how are you? — *¿Cómo estás?*, directions to the bathroom — *¿Dónde está el baño?*, and the important disclaimer that I don't speak Spanish — *No hablo español.* But Janice also taught me far more so that I could pick up important information, even though I pretended not to understand. By no means was I anything near fluent, but I understood more than I let on, which was the plan.

When I finally entered Dr. Rodriquez's office, I was surprised at how small it was — perhaps fifteen feet square and crammed with file cabinets, books, and folders.

"Please sit," he said smiling broadly. "So, how was your trip?"

"Very nice, thank you."

"And your accommodations? It is the same apartment we have used all along for this visiting professorship."

"It's fine," I said. "Very comfortable and gracious."

"Excellent," he said smiling.

The room fell silent as we smiled at each other. After a few seconds, I tried to remember why he had asked me to visit.

"And our city," he said, still smiling, "have you had a chance to see it?"

"Well, only a bit," I said.

"Would you like me to arrange a tour? We have many experts here at the university."

"Oh no, that won't be necessary," I said. "I'd sort of like to discover it myself."

"Ah, yes," he said chuckling. "You Americans are always discovering."

We nodded at each other for several seconds as the awkwardness of the situation crept back. I was certain he had either nothing to say or had something very difficult to say.

"And have you had time to visit your *compatriota* in the Canal Zone?" he said, his smile fading a bit.

"Actually, no," I said. "It's funny. I know that the town of Balboa is only ten miles away, with thousands of Americans. But it might as well be a million miles away. I suppose I'll head over there soon enough."

"I suppose I should mention to you," Rodriguez said, his face suddenly serious, "that the presence of Americans in Panama is not universally perceived as, how do you say? — beneficial."

"Oh?" I replied, feigning curiosity.

"Mmm. Yes," he said shaking his head. "It is unfortunate, but it is still a reality. There is a segment of the population here that is motivated by nationalism. They — how should I put this — they believe that there is no longer a need for colonial governments and that the gains of these colonizing countries should be returned to the indigenous people. Do you see what I mean?"

"I'm not sure," I said squinting.

"Ah, well, then," he said, struggling for the correct wording, "in the case of Panama, there are many here who believe the United States should return the Canal Zone to the Panamanians. I suppose it is that simple, really."

"That's understandable," I said smiling, and seamlessly putting forth my cover as a left-leaning professor. "And I don't blame them. I'm quite sympathetic to their cause, Dr. Rodriguez. I'd just as well give the canal back if it were in my power."

But if I thought my public alignment with the causes of nationalism would assuage him, I was surprised.

"That is an interesting position," he said, "though not one we are accustomed to from Americans. Nevertheless, I feel it is my responsibility to tell you that recently the position you are holding here has been a — how do you say? — a lightning rod."

"In what way?" I asked.

"Ah, well. Your two predecessors experienced resentment from some of the students. And faculty."

"What kind of resentment?"

"Oh, nothing violent, I assure you," he said waving his hand. "Just a spirited exchange in the classroom, for instance. And sometimes in the faculty lounge."

"I see."

"But they do not mean you personal harm, you understand. You simply represent something to them, and they are expressing themselves. It is as simple as that, really. And though you may see signs of the, uh, resentment, I did not want you to feel that your presence here is unwelcome. Indeed we deeply appreciate you and your colleagues' interest in this small — but proud — Central American Republic."

The first day of classes was chaotic. The school year in Panama started the first week of May. I knew the times of day that I was supposed to teach my two courses on English Literature. But I was never given a list of students so I had no idea whether I had ten or fifty students, nor if the students that were in the classroom should be there.

And of course, I did not speak Spanish well enough to navigate the campus. After finding the classroom, I waited outside for the prior class to finish and used the time to re-read my syllabus and fledgling course outline.

On my walk across campus, I had noticed several posters showing the Panamanian flag flying over what looked like the canal. The posters were homemade, and the only words I could read were in English: "Yanqui go home."

The classroom finally emptied, and the teacher, who remained and talked animatedly to two students, introduced himself to me.

"Welcome to Panama," he beamed. "My name is Professor Juan Garcia. I teach history here. I knew your predecessor very well, Tim Duncan. A good man."

"Yes, I hear he was a good teacher and well liked," I said. "Tell me, Juan, if I may: Do teachers receive a list of students prior to their classes? I'm nervous that I won't know who is supposed to be in my class or not."

"Ah, a class list," he said. "No, we are not given a list."

"Well, then, how do I know if a student has come to the wrong class, or that he or she's even supposed to be there?"

Smiling, Juan patted me on the shoulder, "You are just like Tim!"

Sheepishly, I smiled back but pressed ahead, "So, how do we know who's in our class?"

"Whoever shows up for your class is in your class," he said. "Just have them put their names on a piece of paper, pass it around, and return it to you. That is your list."

"Oh, I see."

"And if you don't mind," I said, "can I ask you another question?"

"Of course," he said.

"Do you take attendance? Is that required here?"

"No, I do not take attendance," he said. "Most do not. You, of course, may do so. It is your class and you should run it the way you see fit."

"Well, thank you, Juan. Do you have any last words of advice for me?"

"Just to relax, Nick," he said. "We are better teachers when we relax, would you not agree?"

"Good advice," I said. "*Gracias.*"

"*De nada,*" he replied, smiling broadly.

Thirty-one students showed up for my Introduction to English Literature Class. Even though the class was scheduled to start at 10 a.m., students kept arriving throughout the class period.

I counted only three women in the class. Like most American colleges, the students tended to dress alike. Here, the Panamanian men favored white cotton shirts and dark slacks. The women wore skirts and short-sleeved blouses.

When they weren't coming in late to the class, they were mostly attentive and seemed to understand what I was saying. This particular course was famous — or so I was told — for its immersion in the English language since all of the students were required to understand, if not speak, English.

I wrote an outline for the class on the chalkboard and I held up the books that we'd be using. Then I gave them their first assignment, which was to read The Knight's Tale, the first of the Canterbury Tales and be prepared to discuss it in the next class. With twenty minutes left I asked if anyone had a question.

Two hands shot up. Pointing to one I said, "Yes?"

"Professor Baker, sir. Will you give us a final exam?"

"Good question. Yes, I will be giving a final exam. But don't worry, it won't be too hard," I said smiling. No one smiled back.

I called on the second raised hand.

He stood. "Professor Baker, can you tell us how the New York Yankees are going to do this season?"

Of course, I thought he was kidding, but I noticed every set of eyes was locked onto me.

"I'm sorry," I said slowly, "but I do not follow baseball." There were many disappointed faces.

Feeling very much the stranger, I said, "Well if there are no further questions, you are dismissed. Thank you."

I gathered my papers as the students filed out in groups. Three students hovered nearby. "Professor Baker?" a young man said.

"Yes?"

"Thank you so much for teaching this important course to us. We are proud to have a distinguished American professor in our small country."

"Oh, please," I said, embarrassed by his deference to this fake academic. "It's my pleasure to be here."

"I love English literature," he said.

"Yes, so do I."

"I also write," he said, beaming.

"You do? What kind of writing?" I asked.

"Short stories," he said. "I cannot stop writing. I do it all the time. My *madre* thinks it is such a waste of time."

"Well, you should keep it up."

"Tell me, Professor Baker," he said, "would you look at my writing? It would be an honor to have such a distinguished American professor as you to review some of my writing."

"Sure, I'd be glad to look at it. I assume it is written in English?"

His face froze. "You do not read Spanish?"

"No, I'm sorry I don't."

"All my stories are in Spanish. Aye. I do not write so well in English."

He looked crestfallen.

"Do you know anyone who can translate? Perhaps you can think of someone here at the university who can translate. I would be happy to look at the translation."

"You would?" he said beaming. "There is someone who might be able to translate. Yes, that is possible!"

"What is your name, by the way?"

"Oh, I am so sorry for not introducing myself. Forgive me. My name is Humberto Arias."

"Well, Humberto, if you give me translated copies of your short stories, I would be happy to look at them."

"*Muchas gracias*," he grinned. He shook my hand vigorously and left.

The other two students stepped forward. One was a serious-looking young man with thick, black glass frames.

The other student was a startlingly attractive young woman.

Perhaps it was the combination of physical isolation at Camp Peary or the psychological isolation since my mother's death, but my emotional life was flat. In retrospect, I'm sure I was depressed.

So, I was unprepared for this woman, who took my breath away. She had long black hair, light-olive complexion and penetrating hazel-colored eyes. She looked to be about five feet, two inches, and projected confidence.

"Excuse us, Professor Baker," she said, turning her head toward her partner. "My name is Maria Santiago, and this is my friend Julio Battista."

"Hello," I said.

"Professor, Julio and I were wondering if you would be able to let us accompany you on one of your visits to the Canal Zone. I'm sure you know that many Panamanians are afraid to enter the Canal Zone unless they are visiting families or friends. We are interested in visiting the canal itself. Like many Panamanians, we have never seen it. We apologize in advance for such a request, but perhaps you will take us sometime?"

"Good heavens," I said. "I'm so new here that I haven't visited the Canal Zone myself! I wasn't aware of the rules for non-Americans visiting the canal."

"Not non-Americans," Maria corrected. "Just Panamanians."

For a moment I perceived a flash of emotion in her voice, but it disappeared quickly as she smiled.

"I'd be glad to have you join me for a visit to the canal itself," I said. "It would be my pleasure."

CHAPTER 16

The phone call came just as I was told it would.

"Hey, this is Fred Williams. Is this Nick Baker?"

"Yes, it is."

"Hey, Nick, I'm calling from the Balboa Elks Club. I'm on the educational committee here. I don't know if you're aware or not, but we normally have a reception welcoming the American college professor there at the university."

"Why yes, Fred, I was told you all might call."

"Well, here we are, Nick!" he enthused.

"To be honest, Fred, I've been in Panama for only a week and I haven't even stepped foot in the Canal Zone. Heck, I'm not even sure how to get there from here."

"Don't you worry about that. It's been pretty much the same with your predecessors. My job is to come and pick you up and give a guided tour of the zone. We were kinda hoping that this Saturday would work for you. How's 1 p.m. sound? After the tour of the zone, then we'll head over for a picnic at the lodge. You're our guest of honor! What d'ya think about that, Nick?"

"Jeeze, I'm honored."

"You living at that apartment on 55th Street?"

"Um, yes. The same one the others used."

"Great. See you on Saturday, Nick."

It was distressing how quickly I fell into the routine of being a fake. At Camp Peary, I had been told the students were likely to hold me in awe. Even my professorial colleagues were too deferential, making the entire charade easy. And of course, it was easier to justify living a lie when I was doing important work for my country.

With my first week completed, I sat in my apartment drinking a bottle of Atlas beer. My spy homework consisted of taking careful note of anti-American posters around the campus and identifying the groups listed on them. I also had the opportunity to plant some disparaging comments about the US with my newfound fellow professor Juan Garcia.

"Ha," Juan had laughed when I said I was looking forward to visiting "the colonial outpost" of the Canal Zone. "You sound like your predecessor. He would say things like that. Why is it the Americans who come to this school sound so reasonable, and the one's living a couple of miles away so unreasonable?"

"They're spoiled, Juan. They have too much to lose," I replied.

"Yes," he said smiling, "I suppose that is true."

Fred picked me up right at 1 p.m., just like he said. He was a garrulous man in his late thirties. He drove a new, blue-and-white two-toned Chevrolet Impala and smoked up a storm as we drove through the humid streets of Panama toward the zone.

"Boy, Nick," he said, "you won't believe the difference between the two countries. I mean, it's a real pit on this side. Just look at how these people live," he said, shaking his head.

"And look at those goddamn buses," he said chuckling. "Would you ever get on one of those things? Not on your life!"

Fred was referring to the outrageously painted private buses that plied the streets of the city. They were half-sized buses, packed with people and goods. They sported loud, individualized multi-toned horns that could be heard blocks away.

"Well, they do seem kind of crowded," I said.

"God knows how many diseases those folks have," he said, grimacing.

I looked over to see if he was kidding, but his face was twisted in genuine revulsion.

"Maybe," I said.

Fred kept up this kind of patter until we crossed over into the Canal Zone. The difference was stark.

"Now," Fred said, "isn't this how people are supposed to live?" The streets were clean, the grass was mowed, the houses — many raised with carports underneath — were gently placed into the hilly suburban paradise. Three tanned boys sporting crew cuts zipped by on shiny, fat-tired bikes.

"Jeeze, Fred, it is kind of nice here," I said. "Who are these people? What do they all do?"

"Well, there are basically two kinds of folk who live in the Zone: those that work for the Panama Canal Company — that's the local government that runs the canal; and the other folks are in the military. Heck, we got military bases all over the isthmus."

We drove the long way around Ancon Hill, a jungle-encased bump of surprising height that guarded the southern entrance to Balboa. We passed through a series of very nice neighborhoods, past the edge of the sprawling Albrook Air Force Base, past the zone's ornate administration building, the high school and junior college, and finally down a palm-lined street, into the town of Balboa.

Except for the palm trees — that were inexplicably painted white from the ground to about three feet off the ground — we could have been in any suburb in the US. The cars were all American — Buicks, Chevrolets, Chryslers — and the traffic lights were exactly what you'd expect to see stateside. Downtown Balboa sported a commissary, a club house-cafeteria, a post office, and even a movie theater that backed onto the base of Sosa Hill, a smaller but imposing elephant-grass covered hill.

After driving around the small town, Fred grinned and said, "But I'm sure you'd like to see the main attraction, right?"

"The canal?" I said.

"You got it," he said, grinning.

We drove over to the Miraflores Locks, and I'll admit to feeling a bit giddy about seeing the country's largest public works project. Every American child of my generation had been raised to see this feat of engineering as the capstone of American industrial might and engineering prowess.

"It's really an amazing thing to behold," Fred gushed. "I guess I'm pretty used to it by now, but I still get a hitch in my throat when I see what a marvel of engineering this thing is!"

"Tell me, Fred," I said. "Is it true that an average Panamanian is not able to see the Panama Canal?"

"Good grief, no. Who told you that?"

"Oh, just some kids in my class," I said. "They were complaining that Panamanians can't visit the canal."

"Pure hogwash," he said. "Bunch of crap from those lefties over there. Don't believe it."

I laughed but kept going longer on this thread. There was something that flashed in the student Maria's eyes when she talked about this.

"So it's not restricted then? Any Panamanian can drive over just like you and me right now and visit these locks?"

"Well, not exactly, Nick," he said, sounding very serious. "You wouldn't want to have the entire Panamanian nation coming across into the Zone whenever they felt like it. Hell, that would be a mess! They'd steal us blind."

"But I thought you said they could visit the canal whenever they wanted?"

"I thought you asked whether they can tour the canal, and of course they can. They have set times for Panamanian tours."

"Oh, I see," I said, dropping the subject.

And after a brief ride, we found ourselves in a parking area overlooking the famous Miraflores locks. There was a small freighter departing the lock heading east to the Atlantic port of Colon. A finger of the Pacific could be seen to our immediate left.

"Now, Nick," Fred started on what seemed like an oft-repeated travelogue, "when they first planned the canal, they thought they'd just cut a river connecting the two oceans. Simple as pie. But, you see, the problem is that the Pacific side has a steeper drop than the Atlantic — by about eighteen feet or so — and they'd be creating a constant outflow of water from the Atlantic to the Pacific that would constantly shoal up if you get my drift."

I nodded out of politeness, but I really didn't understand those dynamics.

"They decided that they'd have to create locks here, and another one at Gatun, to either raise or lower the ships. And they needed to create a massive freshwater lake in the middle to allow transit. But the real genius part of this plan — get this, Nick — is that there are no pumps to get water into these locks to raise or lower a ship. It's all done with gravity and water pressure! The ships are always under their own power, but there are little locomotives called 'mules' on the sides of the locks to keep them centered. Amazing, huh?"

I must admit that it seemed like a staggering feat of engineering and was much too complicated for me to fathom. I asked a couple of inane questions about how long it took a ship to traverse, how many ships transited each year, stuff like that, and Fred answered them all very calmly. I couldn't tell whether his answers were correct or not, but I appreciated his enthusiasm and pride.

On the way to the Elks Club, I tried to pay attention to Fred's sight-seeing tips, but I was nervous. The agency's station chief — my boss — had chosen this as our first clandestine meeting.

CHAPTER 17

My back and shoulder were sore by the time I was able to work my way through the crowd at the Benevolent and Protective Order of Elks Club, Balboa, Canal Zone.

"Good luck there, professor" — slap, pat.

"Teach those heathens over there! And watch out for those girls — they sure are wholesome, professor!" — slap, pat, slap.

"Welcome to our part of paradise, young man!" — more painful bonhomie.

There were about fifty men present of varying ages, professions, and waistlines. They seemed tanned, relaxed, and damned happy. Most of them were drinking beer and working their way through a prodigious spread of hamburgers, hot dogs, potato chips, potato salad, and cole slaw. In contrast to the exotic feeling of living in Panama, it felt comfortable to sit with Americans and share a hamburger or hot dog.

After lunch at the head table — and smarting from what now seemed to be welts on my shoulders — there was a brief speech by the head Moose, a tall thin fellow named Georgie, who thanked all those in attendance for the annual welcome and greeting of the visiting American professor at the University of Panama.

And, catching me with a mouthful of hamburger in mid-chew, he said at the podium, "And we'll ask our good professor here to say a few words." He stood away from the podium and joined in the spirited applause from the other elks.

Walking slowly to the podium, I felt the panic attack set in. Standing at the podium while the last of the applause evaporated, I took a deep breath and stumbled forward.

"Gee, this is such an honor for me to be here today," I said. "I want to thank all of you so much for welcoming me with open arms. I especially want to thank Fred for picking me up today and giving me a tour of the Canal Zone. What a wonderful slice of America you have here! When I see what you've accomplished it makes me really proud to be an American!"

Well, I know it wasn't the best speech ever given at the Benevolent and Protective Order of Elks Club, Balboa, Canal Zone, but it wasn't too bad either. Don't ask me where that sop to patriotism came from, but it was there when I needed it, and the applause they gave me — several guys even stood up — confirmed my choice.

After lunch, I mingled with the Elks, who did not seem particularly inclined to go home to their families on such a fine Saturday afternoon in the tropics. The beer flowed freely, and there was much laughter and smoking of cigarettes, cigars, and a few pipes.

And still, I waited to be approached by my station chief. At one point Fred asked if I was ready to go, and I deferred, saying I was having too good a time. Later, I found myself at a table with two men making small talk. After a few minutes, the guy sitting to my left said out of the blue, "Tell me Professor Baker, have you ever been to Paris?"

To my relief, it was the question I had been waiting for all afternoon.

Turning to face my boss — an extraordinarily nondescript man in his late forties — I gave the practiced answer: "No, I've never been to Paris."

The key had been inserted, the lock turned and set. I stared briefly into his eyes, trying to remain nonchalant and professional, and I saw absolutely nothing in return. He did not alter his affect one iota, or twitch an eyelid, or avoid eye contact. The numbing power of his self-restraint caused *me* to break off eye contact.

The group followed a brief thread of conversation around international travel and then petered out. The other participant at the table finally got up to leave.

"You coming, Don?" he said to my station chief.

"Nope," he said. "Think I'll stay a bit longer."

We were left alone at the table. Don toyed with his can of Schlitz while he watched his fellow Elks head out into the sultry mid-afternoon glare.

"How's it going, Haliday?" he said.

"Pretty good, sir," I replied.

"You settled in OK?"

"Yes, sir."

"How's the teaching thing going?"

"It's a lot easier to pull off than I thought. So far, anyway."

"So far?"

"Uh, yes. So far. You know this is my first assignment. Just want to make sure I'm on task."

I'm not sure how he accomplished it in such a brief period of time, but I was feeling very uncomfortable with Don. He spoke in short sentences and seemed to give off virtually no visual readings that I could grasp. Was he nice? Angry? Maniacal? Drunk? I had no idea.

"What's going on at the campus?" he asked.

"Not much that I can see," I said. "There have been some posters denouncing the US control of the canal, but I've been there only a little while."

He took a sip of his beer.

"We don't have forever, Haliday," he said smiling, apparently to convince bystanders that we were having a grand time. "You need to get your ass moving over there. We hear that things are picking up steam with some of the agitators. You need to be on top of that. We haven't received a single communication from you."

"I've only been here a short time."

"Get your ass moving, Haliday. This is serious shit." Then he smiled again. The reprimand and the smile did not go together and further enhanced my impression that Don was going to present a complicated relationship. Plus, he scared the crap out of me.

Fred chatted up a storm when he drove me back to my apartment. I tried to pay attention, but I was greatly unsettled by my brief encounter with Don. He wasn't like anyone else I had met in the agency, but then, I hadn't been in the field before. The pretend spy games running around Norfolk, Virgina, hadn't prepared me for the quiet ferocity I was getting from Don.

"Uh, Maria," I said after class the following week. "Did you and Julio want to go visit the canal? I hadn't forgotten that you wanted to see it."

I decided to move aggressively to insinuate myself into *any* group of students. Out of desperation to appease Don, I remembered that Maria and her friend Julio had asked to visit the canal, so I started with them. They might tell others, who would tell others, who would come to find me.

Maria seemed surprised when I singled her out.

"Oh yes. We would very much like to see the canal. I will tell Julio."

"How about this Saturday?" I said.

"I will need to talk with Julio first."

"Well, I was thinking of Saturday at around 1 p.m. I could pick you two up here at school in front of the admin building. Would that work?"

"Perhaps. I will check with Julio," she repeated. "Thank you so much for remembering."

That week I sat in my apartment correcting papers. I had kept busy during my short stay in Panama, but the loneliness kept creeping in. I had no letters to read from family and friends since I could not tell them where I was. And even if I had wanted to chat with someone, the only close family member was my father — and I was still struggling to engage him.

Sitting on my couch drinking a beer, I concluded that I made a mistake in taking this stupid assignment. There had to be more to life than sitting alone in an apartment in Central America pretending to be a professor so that I could spy on a bunch of kids.

CHAPTER 18

As I waited for Maria and Julio, a thin sheen of perspiration covered my arms, neck, and face. I could feel my shirt sticking to my back as it pressed against the vinyl car seat. I could not get used to the heat and humidity, which manifested in a thin, permanent sheen of perspiration covering any exposed skin. Air conditioning was not generally available in cars back then; we had old-fashioned windows that needed forward propulsion to work.

Maria and her pal agreed to meet me that morning for a visit to the canal, and I worked out the route on a map since I was still not nimble at getting around. They arrived fifteen minutes late, which, as I was learning, was considered punctual in Panama and probably anywhere in the world this close to the equator.

After we exchanged greetings, they joined me in the front seat. In those days the front seat of an American car was as big as a sofa; the back seat could double as a queen-sized bed. Maria sat in the middle and Julio rode shotgun.

He had a small carrying case that held a camera, he said. Maria thanked me a thousand times for taking time out of my busy schedule to drive them to the canal.

Now, perhaps I had been fooling myself about why I chose to escort these two. There might have been another motive. And it was only when my stomach swooned a bit sitting next to Maria that I was even remotely aware of why I had volunteered so quickly.

She sat next to me with her legs pulled up slightly and her hands on her knees. She wore a brightly colored print skirt and a white, short-sleeve blouse. Her black hair was held back by a white headband, giving prominence to her forehead. I couldn't keep my eyes off her and was thankful to be wearing sunglasses.

The drive over to the zone was pleasant. Maria seemed interested in my life and wondered how it was that I chose to teach English Literature. I was shocked at how easily I lied to her about my motivation and passion for literature. Somewhere in the hidden crevices of my conscience, I felt a tad guilty, but that pang was more than compensated for by my awe at the effortlessness involved in doing it.

"I just love the way the words sound when I read great literature," I said. "They're magic really. I just knew I had to teach this to others. Though I'm not sure I'm any good at it."

"Oh, but you are," Maria enthused. "I really like your classes. They are very interesting. Aren't they Julio?"

"Very much so," he said, nodding.

"See?" she said.

"Well, thank you," I said. "Still, I'm hoping I can become a better teacher."

"You are very good," she said, trying to reassure me. "Really."

When we crossed over into the Canal Zone, Maria and Julio stopped talking and stared intensely at the suburban bliss. They sometimes nudged each other to point out something of interest: a new Oldsmobile, a Little League Baseball game, or of all things a police car.

As we drove past the perimeter of Albrook Air Force Base, Julio asked whether he could take a photograph.

"Uh, sure," I said. "Why not?"

Julio dug into his camera bag and came out with a much more

elaborate camera than I expected. It had a telephoto lens, and after adjusting a couple of settings, he clicked away.

Maria pointed to the large jungle-covered hill looming over Balboa. "Is that Ancon Hill?"

I told her it was and pointed out the huge antenna on the top that broadcast the TV channel for residents.

"Oh, I sometimes watch the American television," she said excitedly. "It helps me to learn English. I like Lassie. A very smart dog."

I laughed. "Well, it would be better if we exported something more meaningful to the rest of the world than Lassie."

She turned and stared at me for a moment.

"What is wrong with Lassie?"

"Well, it's just that sometimes the rest of the world sees shows like Lassie and they think we all have families like that, where the mom and dad are, you know perfect. And that we all live on farms, stuff like that."

Maria kept staring at me and I felt unnerved. Meanwhile, Julio clicked away on the other side of the front seat. I tried to keep my eyes on the road, but I could feel her gaze. She finally turned to look at the road and noticed that he was still taking pictures.

"Julio!" she said, in a harsh tone that surprised me. He quickly stopped shooting and put his camera in the bag.

"It's OK, Maria," I said. "He can take photographs."

"He should save film for the canal," she said.

"Yes, of course," I said. "The canal."

We pulled up to the parking area at the Miraflores Locks, and the two of them just sat there staring. I couldn't tell whether they were having a religious experience, a patriotic one, or for that matter were simply disappointed. They just stared at a huge black-and-red tanker as it sat in the lock filled with muddy brown water on the west-bound side. There were several tiny, battleship-gray electric locomotives on each side of the lock that Fred had called "mules," helping the tanker navigate the lock.

"May I?" Julio asked, holding up his camera.

"Sure."

"It is smaller than I thought," Maria finally said.

"Yes, I agree," I said. "But I'm told this is just a fraction of it, of course."

"Of course," she said.

Maria suddenly elbowed Julio and pointed at a worker's shack on the side of the lock. There appeared to be several men talking. Julio clicked away.

"How long does it take for a ship to move through the canal?" Maria asked, turning to me.

And for the first time — it was a fleeting impression and afterwards I could not recollect why it struck me — I felt Maria was manipulating me. I remember smiling as I looked at her face, radiant in the tropical sunlight. In what must have been a nervous tic, she gently bit the inside of her lip.

"Gee, Maria, that's a good question," I said. "I'm afraid I don't know the answer. I can find out for you."

"Oh no, that is not necessary," she said. "I was wondering, that is all."

"Someone told me it takes at least twelve hours, but I hope I remembered correctly."

"I see," she said.

"And another thing that's interesting," I said, parroting Fred, "is that a ship can only traverse the canal with a pilot. They are never driven by their own captain. They have to turn over control of the ship to a pilot, who meets them at the entrance on a small launch."

"Interesting," she said. I noticed Julio was changing the film.

"Do you want to get out and take a walk?" I asked.

"Oh no," she said. "We are fine here."

The three of us stared at the huge ship that seemed to have no room on its sides, sitting in a concrete channel, looming above us. From our angle, it seemed like the ship was sitting motionless on land.

As the lock gates slowly opened, the tanker moved incrementally forward toward the Pacific Ocean. We had been there for thirty minutes and the tanker seemed to barely move.

"It is very complicated," Maria said.

"Yes," I said. "Seems that way. You know, I'm sorry you haven't been able to visit the canal before. I feel bad about that. It's your canal."

Maria turned again in her seat and stared at me.

"Why do you say that?" she said.

"Well, it's your land, isn't it? I mean we're in Panama, aren't we?"

After a pause, her face grew taut and serious, and she said, "Are you being provocative?"

I laughed. "Maria, I'm not trying to be disrespectful. I'm just telling you that it's a shame that you and Julio have never seen the canal. We Americans built the canal and are operating it, but as far as I'm concerned, this belongs to Panama, and I'd just as well they consider giving it back sooner rather than later."

Now Julio looked at me as well. I felt the dampness of my shirt on the seat back and tried to shift my weight.

"I hope you are not making fun of us," she said.

"Good grief, no," I protested. "Does every American have to agree with the policies of its government? I'm just telling you and Julio that it's a shame we have to keep Panamanians from their own canal. It's not right. What can I say?"

"Hmm," Maria said, turning to watch the rusty-red tanker inch its way toward the vast Pacific Ocean.

The ride back through the Canal Zone was tense; Maria seemed standoffish and Julio just stared at the well-kept lawns, new cars, and towheaded American kids playing baseball. When we crossed back into Panama they seemed to brighten, and Maria made a point of thanking me again for the visit. I dropped them off at a street corner to catch a bus, and I drove home, smiling at the memory of Maria sitting next to me.

CHAPTER 19

There were times when I actually believed I was a college professor. I would lecture on Yeats, for instance, and ask the class questions. They would ask me questions and I would answer them. It's so easy to lie when you have the full backing of the United States government.

And Maria started lingering after class, which I found interesting and thrilling. Sometimes she had Julio with her, and other times she was alone. We made small talk mostly, and I could not tell whether she was flirting or just trying to befriend her professor for a better grade. These things happen.

I was also coming to grips with the complexity of different subcultures in Panama. The nuances of behavior, tradition, and language were complicated. There was the Spanish-speaking, Roman Catholic mestizo majority; the English-speaking, Protestant Antillean blacks; tribal Indians, like the Cuna of the San Blas Islands. And of course, there were smaller groups of Indians, Jews, Greeks, and Chinese.

Maria was mestizo, I guessed. Her light brown skin and dark hair seemed to put her in this group. She seemed to carry herself — like many of the students in my class — with a kind of privileged bearing. I could not put my finger on it, but she seemed quite confident of her place in life.

One day I asked her why there were so few women in the school.

"Oh, that is because a woman should not be interested in the university. It is frowned upon. We are supposed to be *madres* — mothers, yes?"

"Then how come you are here?"

"I don't want to be a mother now," she laughed. "I am too young."

"How old are you?" I couldn't resist.

"Very young," she said laughing, throwing her head back, flicking her hair.

"*¿Cuántos años tienes?*" I asked, slipping into Spanish.

"*¿Por qué?*" she said, squinting.

It was at that moment that I recognized — perhaps she did too — that we had crossed that delicate line between normal discourse and into flirtation. It was the universal dance, I suppose.

"I just want to know," I said. "It's a harmless question."

"*Veintiuno,*" she said nervously, and it occurred to me she was uncertain about my reaction. Maybe she thought she was too young, or too old for that matter.

"Twenty-one? Ha," I said.

"Why do you laugh?" she said, appearing embarrassed.

"Well, I'm not that much older than you."

"So?" she said.

"So," I said.

"How old are you, Professor Baker? Now I must know."

"Senorita Santiago," I said, now parrying back with the same mock formality, "I'm twenty-three years old. Not much older than you."

"I see," she said, flicking her head. Her long, luxurious black hair swung out to the side, and she just glided away with her books held tight against the curve of her hips.

Of course, I was embarrassed to be flirting with her. I could only imagine what Don would have said if he'd seen the interchange. Good old Don, my station chief, and likely tormentor. He needed vital information and I had none to give. Instead, I was spending my time flirting shamelessly with one of my students. This spy stuff was so complicated.

My impromptu hallway conversations with my fellow professor Juan Garcia were uneventful. It was difficult to corner any of them besides Juan. A couple of times he seemed in a hurry and waived to me as he rushed down the hall. Yet on several other occasions, we chatted for forty-five minutes or so.

"So, Nick," he finally said one afternoon, "remember I asked whether you would be interested in visiting our little group to discuss American-Panama relations. Is that still possible for you?"

"Of course, Juan, that sounds like a great idea. I'd be glad to join you. Just tell me when and where."

"You Americans are so direct," he laughed. He offered to pick me up the following night and take me to a gathering of his academic friends.

"My pleasure," I enthused. "I'll be ready."

He was a half hour late the following evening, but I was slowly acclimating to the concept of timeliness in equatorial lands. We chatted aimlessly in the car, and I was a little nervous but also intrigued by my impending brush with the Panamanian intelligentsia. Was he taking me to a gathering of a communist cell? A Cub Scout merit badge ceremony? A film club?

We parked in front of a two-story residential building that I recognized as being near the university.

"You will feel very much at home, Nick," Juan said. "Most of the people here are professors at the university."

We entered the small apartment and, judging by the group there, we were late to the drinking party. There were eight people, only two of them women. It seemed that everyone was smoking cigarettes and the air seemed layered in smoky cirrus clouds. In the Panamanian custom, I shook every single person's hand.

And of course, the conversations were in Spanish. Juan introduced me to everyone, but I could only remember two people's names: Philippe, because he was very chubby, and Gloria, who had large breasts. Not that she exposed them in a lascivious way, but leaning forward to make a point, her puny bra was not capable of holding back the sheer weight of flesh.

I was proud of myself for not staring at her chest, but several other male members of our rag-tag party could be seen periodically tilting their head or shifting their gaze to follow the twin pillars of Gloria.

The folks closest to my chair were kind enough to speak to me in English, while others continued animated conversations in Spanish — none of which I could understand. I scanned for some of the people in Don's lineup, or for other Europeans but came up blank. So much for my hope of running into a Soviet Bloc connection. I had been warned that communist agitation in Panama was likely coming from east European operatives from Bulgaria, Poland, and East Germany. Russia did not have diplomatic relations with Panama.

The guests were drinking large quantities of rum — rum at room temperature in small glasses; rum mixed with Coca-Cola and ice; rum straight out of the freezer in small shot glasses, and even rum mixed with milk.

It did not take long for someone to confront me on the stance of the US toward Panama.

"So, Professor Nick," one young man to my left said between furious puffs of a cigarette, "what do you Americanos have against Panamanians anyway? We are a small, puny people."

"No, only you are puny, Stefano," Juan shot back.

"I don't think Americans have anything against Panamanians," I said gamely.

"Tell us then," the woman Gloria said, interrupting the other speaker, "why it is permissible to pay a Panamanian worker at the canal less money than an American worker if they do the same work?"

"It's not permissible," I said. "It's wrong."

"You believe it is wrong?" she asked, surprised.

"Yes, of course," I said. "I suppose it's a vestige of colonialism. It's still wrong."

"Perhaps it's racism," said another man sitting to Gloria's right.

"It could be," I said. "I would hope not, but it is possible."

"Why do you make your Negroes live apart from the white people in the Canal Zone?" another man asked me.

"I don't know about that. Do they segregate Negroes there?" I asked.

"Of course," Gloria said. "Rainbow City and Paraiso are places for the Negroes. You should visit them. And be ashamed."

"Gloria!" Juan shouted. "*¿Pero qué te pasa?*"

"It's OK," I said, downing a huge gulp of milk and rum. "Gloria is correct. I should be ashamed. I'm not proud of many things my country does. But it is still my country."

"Of course it is," Juan said, giving Gloria a stern glance.

The evening then became a blur of rum, spirited debate, more rum, and laughter. Juan kept filling my glass with the milk-rum mixture, and oddly, it tasted good. I couldn't figure out whether he wanted to get me drunk or just sedate me against the anti-American diatribes.

"You are not like other Americans," Juan said at one point during the evening, smiling broadly. "You do not argue. Your predecessor argued, but you do not. You just agree. It is hard to argue when you agree with everything."

"But I don't want to argue," I said. "Why is it necessary to argue?"

"We are professors. The intelligentsia of this small country. Besides teaching, we argue. What else is there?"

I chuckled, tossing down another gulp of the rum. "Why argue when you can agree? There is little to defend about the Canal Zone. We should be turning it over to Panama to run. Simple as that. I wish I could do more to make that happen, but I'm just a simple professor."

Juan threw his head back and laughed loudly, then turned and spoke in Spanish to the fellow next to him. The two exchanged a few words, laughing between themselves.

Turning to me, Juan said, "He thinks you are a Russian spy! A true Marxist. 'No American speaks like that!' You are funny, Nick."

He poured me another rum.

"But surely you don't think Panamanians can operate the canal? Americans think we are too lazy," Gloria said, eavesdropping on our conversation.

"And corrupt," said the fellow next to Juan.

"But we *are* corrupt," said Juan and everyone laughed.

"Well, so we are corrupt, but what country is not?" the man persisted. "Does it mean we cannot operate a canal? We already do much of the work there anyway."

"Have you thought of a strike?" I said.

"What kind of strike?" said Gloria leaning forward intently. Several participants shifted their gaze momentary to look at her chest.

"A strike by the Panamanian workers at the canal," I said. "Strike for a couple of days, just to show them that you are serious about equal compensation at the very least. I bet that would get their attention."

Several animated conversations, all in Spanish, started around me.

"You have surprised them with your attitude," Juan said. "And you have surprised me. Are you sure you're not a Marxist?"

And before I knew it the conversation turned unavoidably to baseball. Several of the men pressed me hard on two players: Hector Lopez of the Kansas City Athletics, and Humberto Robinson, a pitcher for the Milwaukee Braves. Both were Panamanians born in Colon.

I knew a little about baseball but could only list a handful of top players by name, and certainly not these two players. It didn't stop them pressing me and we spent the rest of the evening drinking rum and talking baseball.

By the time I got in Juan's car to go home I was a little drunk.

"You perhaps had too much rum, my friend," Juan said. "I'm sorry. I should have been more careful."

"Don't be silly," I slurred, trying to crane my neck out the window to get some fresh air.

The drive seemed like it took forever, and I fought the spinning sensation that was making me feel ill. Juan kindly helped me up to my apartment. He offered to come in, but I told him I was fine, which I was for about five minutes. But after lying down in bed and feeling the world whizzing around me like a psychotic pinwheel, I stumbled to the toilet where, with great gusto, I emptied my stomach.

Another hard day in the service of my country.

Two days later I was summoned to Dr. Rodriguez's office by a young student courier. I sat in his outer office, trying to read a Spanish-language magazine on the coffee table, while his secretary hummed a song to herself.

His door finally opened, a visitor departed, and I stood up so he could see me.

"Ah, Professor Baker," he said beaming, "please come in."

He closed the door and I sat across from his small, cluttered desk.

"So, how are your classes?"

"Very good, thank you. I really enjoy the students and they seem to enjoy the material. So far, so good."

"Are the students well behaved?" he asked, smiling.

"Yes, of course, they are. Have you heard that there's a problem?"

"No, no," he said, shaking his head in reassurance. "To the contrary. We have heard nothing negative."

"Oh, good," I said. "You had me worried."

"But," he said, "there are rumors."

"Rumors? Rumors of what?"

"Of disturbances," he said, still smiling. It finally occurred to me that Rodriguez smiled whenever he spoke, regardless of the nature of the conversation. I found it unnerving.

"Please, President Rodriguez, can you be more specific? I'm not entirely sure what you're talking about. What kind of 'disturbances'"?

"The agitators are stirring up trouble everywhere in Panama," he said. "And of course they always find a fertile home at the university. Ah," he sighed wistfully, "why is it that the educated young are so eager to get involved in these events?"

"What events?" I persisted.

"*Una manifestación* — a protest," he said frowning for the first time.

"About what?"

"The canal," he said, smiling again. "It is always the canal. And American imperialism. Always the two. Please, I hope I do not offend."

"No, of course not," I said. "When is the demonstration?"

Rodriguez reached over his desk and grabbed a two-sided flyer that looked like a newspaper, with large headlines, pictures, and articles. He handed it to me.

"I cannot read this, can you help me," I said.

"It is a newspaper put out by the agitators," he said. "It is full of the usual charges — that the canal is Panamanian territory and yet we have no rights in the Canal Zone. That the Americans treat us like slaves there. The same charges. Of course, it creates a patriotic reaction for people here. We are a small country, but still proud, you understand."

"So when is the demonstration?"

"Friday," he said. "Here on campus. We will cancel classes, of course."

I turned the flyer around and scanned the articles. There was a large photo at the top of the page, showing the Miraflores Locks. In the photo, several men were standing around one of the locomotive mules on the lock platform.

"Can you help me," I said. "What is this story about?"

He took the sheet from me and peered at it for a moment. "This issue is a sore point for Panamanians," he said. "The canal government pays Americans who work there a higher wage than the Panamanians. Even though they do the same work. This article shows a picture of some Panamanian workers and an American working side-by-side. The words under the photograph say, 'Although the American worker and his Panamanian compatriots perform the same duties, the Panamanians are paid slave wages. We demand equal treatment.'"

Rodriguez chuckled slightly and shook his head as he looked up at me. "I wonder how they got this photograph?" he said. "You must admit they are resourceful."

I took the sheet back and looked closely at the photograph. I recognized the photo. Julio took the shot from my car. Maria had pointed something to him while sitting next to me.

They probably thought I'd never see this stupid flyer. My humiliation — and anger — at being manipulated by Maria was offset somewhat by the professional glee at stumbling upon a group I was sent to target in the first place. Now, at least, I had a starting point and I could give something back to Don.

"May I take this with me?" I asked.

"Of course," he said, smiling again.

I folded it and stuffed it into a book.

"Oh, and it would be best if you were not at the university on Friday. I'm sure you understand that no harm will come to you here, but you're the only American professor on the campus, and we can never tell where emotions will run. It is best if you remain away. You understand, of course?"

"Good advice," I said.

"And also, please be warned that you may be provoked in your classes," he said. "It happened with your predecessor, and he handled it very well. We recommend you do not answer any questions not germane to the subject you are teaching. Sometimes the more radical students cannot resist the temptation to bait the only American here. It is harmless, but a fact of life, unfortunately."

"Thanks for the warning."

I left and walked across the campus to my car, feeling for the first time more self-conscious than normal. The heat and humidity had soaked my shirt by the time I got to my car. I sat in the front seat for a second, trying to steel myself for the craziness that was about to start.

CHAPTER 20

The first thing I did after dropping a pile of student papers on the kitchen table, was to open the patio slider, walk over to the twelve-inch terra cotta flower pot holding my resurrected hibiscus, and move it from the right side of my balcony railing to the extreme left.

I peered out into the gathering darkness of this middle-class residential section of the city. A dog barked nearby, and I heard the peal of laughter from two young children. Lights flickered through the thick foliage. I could smell onions frying somewhere.

My puppy-love pain be damned; the assignment was in play and I finally had something to give Don. The flowerpot was my signal that I was going to make a dead drop tomorrow.

I grabbed a beer out of the fridge and sat at the small dining room table, staring at the pile of papers to grade. I felt that familiar pulse of loneliness and self-pity that had seemed to follow me through my short life.

The following morning, I got to the university earlier than normal and walked around the campus. It was Thursday, the day before the big demonstration, and I noticed many more posters.

The mood on campus seemed festive and electric. Lots of students said hello to me as I walked by, so I didn't feel particularly threatened.

I entered the men's room on the second floor of the main building and mercifully found the designated first stall open. I closed the door, took out my note to Don — no cipher and codes, straight English — and stuck it in the space behind the toilet bowl. I made sure no piece of it protruded, then flushed the toilet and left.

An unidentified runner was to pick up the note and get it to Don. If he wanted to write back to me, there was an apartment window a block from my house that had its blinds always closed. If the blinds suddenly were open, I was to check the dead drop as soon as feasible.

Pretty simple stuff.

Of course, if Don or I needed to get hold of each sooner there were telephone protocols to follow.

I was looking forward to seeing Maria in class that day. I had rehearsed my speech to her.

But she skipped class, which threw me. She had perfect attendance.

"Julio," I said after class, "where was Maria today?"

"No sé," he shrugged.

"OK, thanks," I said.

I took a walk early that evening through the neighborhood and glanced at the apartment window. The blinds were open.

Now it was my turn to pick up a return message, the only problem being that classes were cancelled tomorrow, and I had been strongly encouraged to stay away from the campus. I decided to get into the admin building early and pick up my drop.

That night I dreamed of my mother. I remember it vividly because I woke up at 2 a.m. with the unsettling feeling that she was in the room. It bothered me so intensely that I finally had to get up and read a book just to take my mind off her. I fell asleep on the couch and did not wake up until 8 a.m.

I rushed out of the apartment and made it to the university by 9 a.m. The campus was nearly empty at that time of day. In the bathroom stall, I searched the back of the toilet bowl looking for the return note. I couldn't find it. Feeling stupid, I got down on my knees and kept poking around the bowl on all sides. Nothing.

In frustration, I replayed the dead-drop directions and wondered if I had missed something.

The men's room door opened, and I heard someone step into the bathroom and stop. That was unusual — I would have expected him to go right to the urinal or the other stall, but not stop.

The adrenal gland did its job, and I felt the immediate consequences of its release in my bloodstream: my heart jumped, my breathing shallowed, and I felt little pricks of electricity in my chest.

Had I been followed? Was it an overzealous agitator who had seen the American professor across campus and followed him? Hell, was it the janitor?

I made a shuffling sound with my feet to communicate someone was in the stall, but still, the person did not move. I was about to bend over to look under the stall when I heard the person walk slowly up to the door of my stall.

I looked down and could see a shadow of the person standing in front of the stall. My imagination took a dark turn and I kicked myself for not bringing the pistol. They told me not to carry it, but dammit, I was about to be gun downed! I imagined three little holes from the assassin's rounds as they penetrated the flimsy metal door and ripped through my chest.

Then, of all things, there were three distinct raps on the stall door. Very modest taps, barely audible above the din from my thumping heart.

Regaining a modicum of composure, I opened the stall door.

A man, perhaps in his thirties, stood in front of me. He wore a traditional Panamanian white shirt with intricate patterns woven into it. He had dark blue slacks, dark shoes. His face was blank, and I could not read his expression.

He just looked at me and I looked at him. I still didn't know if he was going to shoot me or begin to clean the toilet.

I flinched first and said, "Si?"

He kept staring at me, and I concluded that something bad was going to happen. The man reached into his back pocket and pulled out an envelope. Without saying a word, he handed it to me, turned, and left the men's room. I stood motionless in exactly the same spot I had for the last minute in the stall. I heard his footsteps fade away down the empty hallway.

It took me a few seconds to piece together what happened: the dead-drop courier was just as startled to find me in the stall as I was to find him standing outside the stall.

He obviously saw me enter the bathroom. While he certainly saved me another trip back to the stall later, I was troubled by the fact that he departed from the established protocols. The courier should *never* be able to identify the recipient of the drop since if they are compromised, the recipient can be compromised.

This sloppy courier simply decided, after verifying that I was a clueless American, to pony up with the envelope.

I would mention that to Don next time I saw him.

I ripped open the envelope and read the message. It was printed in primitive block letters: "1 p.m. today, Balboa cafeteria."

I reread it several times, though its brevity was almost laughable. I held the corner of the notepaper and lit it with a match. When the flame reached my fingertips I dropped it in the toilet where it hissed plaintively. I did the same with the envelope, though that took two matches. I flushed my first secret missive down the dark sewer.

The downtown area of Balboa in the Canal Zone had the warm, homey feel of a TV show like Adventures with Ozzie and Harriet, only with palm trees. Following the main boulevard from the Administration Building, you were led to a small downtown. The Balboa cafeteria sat at the base of Sosa Hill, and on one side of the green was the commissary, with the post office on the other.

It was pleasant, idyllic even. The public spaces were all landscaped and mowed tightly. I parked and sauntered into the cafeteria. I slid a tray on the stainless-steel rail, grabbing a hamburger, French fries, and a Coke. I did not see Don, so I took a table and devoured my American hamburger with great pleasure. Before I could dig into my fries, Don appeared next to me.

"Hey, aren't you that American professor working at the university in Panama?" he said loudly.

"Yes," I said. "How did you know?"

"I think we met at the Elks Club," he said.

Standing, I shook his hand. "Nick Baker, good to meet you."

"Don Templeton, nice to see you again. Mind if I join you?"

"Not at all. Take a seat."

Don sat across from me, nursing a black cup of coffee in a thick, glossy white ceramic cup and saucer.

"So," Don said smiling broadly, but in a lower voice, "what's up? Got anything for us?"

"Yes," I said grabbing a fry and stuffing it into my mouth. "I stumbled onto two students who are involved with the leftists."

"What do you mean 'involved?'" he said.

"They asked me to take them for a visit to the canal. Said they weren't allowed to visit by themselves. I took them one Saturday. The guy had a camera and he took some pictures. And that was that. This week the president calls me in to his office and tells me there's a big anti-American demonstration planned for today."

"Yep, it's set for later today," Don said nodding.

"Well, the president shows me a propaganda leaflet with a big picture of Panamanian and US workers at one of the canal locks. It's some kind of controversy about equal pay. Anyway, I look at the picture and it's one of the photos the kid had taken from my car. They used me to get these stupid photos."

"Little shits," Don said, smirking. "How did you handle it with the kids?"

"Well, I haven't seen the main one yet. She skipped class. She's pretty sharp. The other kid — the photographer — looks like he's just taking orders."

"A girl? What's her name?" Don said, grabbing a paper napkin and taking a fountain pen out of this shirt pocket.

"Maria Santiago. His name is Julio Battista."

As Don wrote their names in block letters on the napkin, the fountain pen bled profusely, blotching some of the letters.

"Crap," Don said absently. He put away his pen and reread their names to me.

"Good," he said. "Now listen, Haliday, you've got to get involved in that girl's group. You know the drill. Do whatever it takes. Seduce the girl if you have to, just get inside that group."

"I'm not going to seduce her," I said with probably too much umbrage. "That's silly."

"For god's sake, you're a field agent, Haliday. If you've got to seduce a college girl to get the goods, then it's all in a day's work. What the hell are they teaching you guys at Peary these days? Jesus."

Maybe I had led a protected life of upper-middle class splendor that didn't prepare me for the simple binary math of good guys-vs.-bad guys espionage. Don's approach seemed crass.

But it was no good to argue with him. Besides, I was embarrassed and pissed off at Maria for setting me up, and it didn't do any good to try to treat her like a prima donna.

"Listen, Haliday," he said. "We're getting word that they're really getting organized over there. I've got Washington worried to death that if we don't head this thing off we're going to have a heap of trouble. We're not losing this canal like the Brits and Frogs did at the Suez."

"I'll do my best," I said, draining the last of my Coke.

"Spare me the Boy Scout promises," he said. "The only thing you need to do is penetrate that group and find out who the ringleaders are. That's it. Pure and simple. Anything less than that and you've failed."

"Why is it," the bad Nick said before he could be controlled, "that whenever I talk to you I feel like crap?"

"Grow up," Don said smiling and rising from the table, "and get your goddamn job done."

Large windows in the cafeteria looked down upon the small square. I watched Don walk out of the building, across the street, and into his car. He drove away in a rush, not bothering to use hand signals or directionals, and nearly plowed into a Ford station wagon that honked loudly.

Maybe I did need to grow up.

CHAPTER 21

The demonstration was larger than they had predicted; more than 5,000 people turned out to shout down American imperialism and burn Uncle Sam in effigy. They torched a couple of American flags, which is always better than torching a couple of Americans.

I was glad to see Maria in my next class. She nodded when she came in and sat in her usual spot. I was on guard for disruptions targeted at me, the token American on campus. But it seemed like a normal class. One student talked quite passionately about Shakespeare's Sonnet 18 "Shall I compare thee to a summer's day?"

As the students filed out afterward, I tried to catch Maria's eye, but she seemed intent on avoiding me. Did she think I knew about the photograph? Had something changed?

"Maria," I called. "*Un momento por favor.*"

Threading through the departing students she stood in front of me.

"I thought English was to be spoken in the class?" she said. "Now you speak Spanish."

"Class is over," I said.

"Ah, yes, it is," she said.

"I missed you last Thursday."

"I was not feeling well."

"Are you well now?"

"Yes, very much so, thank you."

"Did you have a chance to attend the demonstration last Friday here?" She looked surprised.

"Perhaps," she said.

"Well, I was wondering why you didn't ask me to attend with you?"

She made a short, sharp laugh, flicking her head slightly.

"That would not have been good."

"Well, I was just wondering because, as you know, I had been helping the cause."

"I do not understand," she said, clearly confused. "I am not able to understand you."

Turning to my notebook I pulled the folded flyer out and spread it onto my desk. All the students had left so I felt comfortable confronting her.

Pointing to the photograph I said, "Julio did a nice job of this after you were able to point out what to shoot."

Maria blushed; her neck grew blotchy and she bit the inside of her lip as she stared at the flyer. When she looked up at me, I couldn't read her expression. She was either really pissed off at me or feeling stupid at being caught, or both.

Instead of answering me she simply shrugged and waved her right hand in a careless kind of dismissal and turned to leave.

I reached out and grabbed her wrist; I could feel her muscles and tendons tighten as she yanked it away from me.

"What do you want," she said.

"Listen, Maria," I said, trying to soften the moment, "I just wanted to tell you that I'm glad I could help you and Julio. You could have told me why you wanted to visit the canal and I would have helped you. I'm embarrassed at how we treat Panamanians. My sympathies are with the Panamanian people. Next time you want help with something like this, you can turn to me. No questions asked. Do you understand?"

As was her habit at difficult moments, she simply shrugged, turned without speaking, and walked away. After she exited the classroom I put the flyer back in my notebook and gathered my materials. I was struck by her steely demeanor. She agreed to nothing, confirmed nothing, and left me standing there like an idiot.

Did she believe me? Could she trust me? Would she take my offer to someone higher up, or could this little panther in the pleated skirt see right through my flimsy cover?

And then I waited. Either Maria was going to be my entry into her group, or it was going to be a dead end.

Three days later I dutifully noted the blinds were up in the apartment down the street. Standing in the bathroom stall the next day I opened the envelope. The message from Don was simple: "So?"

The following week in class, during a discussion on William Wordsworth, a student that I was not familiar with raised his hand.

"Professor Baker," he said, "is William Walker a hero in America?"

"I beg your pardon?" I said.

"Is William Walker a hero in your country?" he repeated.

I quickly scanned the classroom looking at the students' faces. Some students were just as confused as I was, but others seem to be smirking, and a couple — like Maria — were upset.

"I don't understand your question," I said. "Who is William Walker? And who are you?"

"My name is Rodolfo," he said.

"Rodolfo, I have no idea who William Walker is. If he has nothing to do with English Literature, then I don't think it's appropriate for this class."

"Ah, but he must be a great American," Rodolfo insisted, his mocking tone quite clear now. "He has done great things to make all

Americans proud."

Someone called Rodolfo's name in a stern voice. I looked to see Maria giving an icy stare to the questioner. He turned to look at her, then faced me again smirking. I heard several chuckles in the class.

"Well, if that's all the questions then class is over for today," I said hurriedly.

Some of the students filing out seemed embarrassed and made a point of saying goodbye. Maria filed out without acknowledging me.

That evening I drove to the Canal Zone and visited the library there. I had no clue who or what William Walker was.

The reference librarian, an older woman with snow-white hair, was at first just as clueless. "William Walker," she kept repeating out loud as if she was waiting for his name to unlock something.

I followed her over to the card index files, and right before she reached for one of the wooden drawers, she said, "Oh, do you mean William Walker of Nicaragua? That Walker?"

"Jeeze, I don't know. It could be."

"Yes, I bet that's who you're interested in," she said almost to herself. She puttered around some index cards, and then led me down the stacks of books until she found what she was looking for.

"Here," she said triumphantly, "you'll find something about Mr. Walker in this one."

And so I did. William Walker, it seems, was a nineteenth century adventurer from Tennessee. In 1853 he assembled a group of 170 men along with some field guns and invaded Baja, California, to declare himself president of that area. The Mexican Army sent him packing. But in 1855 he set his sights, apparently, on Nicaragua. He invaded with a small group of Americans, and took control of the country. In 1856 the US State Department recognized his government. Walker quickly rescinded Nicaragua's prohibition on slavery.

Walker's actions frightened the rest of Central America, and a small coalition of forces invaded Nicaragua and forced him out. Back in the states he again gathered a small armed force and reentered Nicaragua. Forced out yet again, he spent the next three years building another force and landed in neighboring Honduras in 1860, planning to invade by land. But he was arrested this time and was finally dispatched forever by a firing squad.

So this is what Rodolfo was up to. Calling out American imperialism at its finest.

Rodolfo was not in the next class and I wondered if he was really an English Lit student after all. He probably attended that single class just to harass me.

I handed back some papers and asked several students to read their papers. Maria was one of the students and she seemed slightly nervous reading her piece on Dickens.

At the end of the class, Maria approached me.

"Hi," she said.

"How are you doing? I haven't seen much of you lately."

"I've been very busy," she said.

"Where was Rodolfo today? I was looking forward to chatting with him."

With a dismissive flick of her head, she said, "Pay no attention to Rodolfo. He is not even in your class."

"Yes, I gathered that," I laughed.

"He will not be back," she said.

I decided to press more aggressively. With the languid pace of life here I could be waiting for months before Maria decided to introduce me to anyone else in her group.

"You know, Maria, I've been here a while and I've never seen Old Panama," I said. "I was wondering if you'd be interested in showing me around as a tour guide. It would be much better seeing sites like this from you rather than someone from the Canal Zone."

"Perhaps," she said carefully.

"Good, how about this Saturday? Tell me where I can pick you up. It'll just be for a couple of hours. Get you back home by early afternoon."

"Maybe," she said.

"Oh come on, Maria," I said teasing. "Sightseeing with your professor? How much more exciting can it be?"

"Mmm," she said.

I decided to just shut up and let the offer marinate.

Maria looked at her watch. "I must go," she said.

"So?" I said. "What time this Saturday?

And for perhaps the first time in a while a smile flickered across Maria's face. I had rarely seen her smile, and it was clear why. She appeared both beautiful and vulnerable at the same time. I don't think Maria liked being seen as vulnerable.

"You are persistent, Professor Baker."

"And persuasive," I said smiling.

"OK," she smiled again. "I will show you *Panama Viejo*."

She wrote down a street address and told me she would be out front at 1 p.m. on Saturday.

CHAPTER 22

Panama's rainy season started in May. It did not resemble any rain I was familiar with. The sky would shine bright blue interspersed with billowy, cotton-candy clouds grouped here and there. Suddenly, the sky would open in a downpour of warm raindrops the size of marbles pounding everything in sight.

You could see the rain approaching in vertical, gray sheets. Behind the rain was a blue sky. During these random downpours, water roared down gutters and swamped streets in twelve inches of water.

Then it would stop as if someone hit a switch, and the sky glowed that special tropical blue as if nothing had happened. The air would hang humid as if you were covered in a plastic shower curtain.

Friday night I stood inside the slider on my apartment porch and watched the water pour from the sky. The rain bent branches and filled my flowerpot to the brim. And just as quickly, it stopped. The only sound was the exhausted aftermath of water dripping from roofs, trees, and bushes.

There was something comforting about the drenching, warm rain that evening and I luxuriated in it. Breathing in the pungent aroma of tropical foliage and watching the draping leaves of a mango tree near the porch, I fought off the loneliness that had been plaguing me forever.

And I was growing fond of this odd little country — the earnest students trying to understand the poetry and prose of long-dead Europeans, my neighbors on the street who smiled broadly and waved when I took my walks, the officious but humane university president, and even the weather was growing comfortable.

That evening I finally forced myself to read Humberto's short story. He had asked someone to translate it into English, which I found impressive. It was carefully typed and held together by brass pins that ran through three punched holes on the left side.

I grabbed a beer and sat at the kitchen table.

The cover sheet read, "The Iguana, by Humberto Arias."

I sighed and turned to the first page. I took a swig of beer at the same time and a huge drop of condensation slid off the bottle and onto the first page, smudging several letters.

"Damn," I said, blotting it with my t-shirt.

Then I started reading.

"The dirt road meandered up the hillside and into the village of Santa Ana like it had for many years, perhaps for centuries. It was dusty in the dry season and muddy in the rainy season, but it was the only lifeline that connected Santa Ana to the rest of the country and the world beyond."

OK, I thought. Nice start.

"Clara de Gonzalez placed her hands on her hips and sighed. It was a half-mile to the mountain stream where she washed her family's clothes on the large flat rocks. Now, having carried the damp clothes back to the house she was ready to hang them on the brown rope that hung between the papaya tree near the back door to the bean tree next to the shed.

Clara's back ached, and she took a moment to look out over the green-carpeted valley, while she gathered her strength.

She heard the deep sound of a hummingbird and smiled as the black-headed bird nervously stopped and started, investigating the red blossoms on the hibiscus bush.

Clara bent down to grab the first piece of clothing, her husband's old white t-shirt now stained with age, mango juice and ash from the fire pit. *She gently unrolled it from the ball she had rolled at the stream to squeeze out the water and lay it over the line. The cool sea breeze from the coast had just started up and she watched the t-shirt lift and wave itself in the sunlight.*

It was then, out of the corner of Clara's eye, that she caught sight of the iguana lurking at the edge of her lawn, its head bobbing up and down as the animals did when they were mating.

Clara stood up slowly to look at the iguana. It was not just that she recognized the potential for a meal for the family, or that it was of a handsome size, or even that it seemed to be staring directly at her. No, what caught Clara's eye — and caused her to gasp — was its color.

This iguana was a solid, deep blue color, with two tiny black circles near the tip of its tail.

Iguanas are not supposed to be blue.

Clara looked away for a moment to remain calm, her heart beating rapidly. She returned her gaze to the animal, hoping it had disappeared.

Indeed, a blue iguana sat not thirty feet from her, bobbing its head.

'Aiy,' she said out loud. It could only be a very bad omen, and she quickly scanned the front yard looking for signs of her two boys and daughter. 'Aiy', she said again, frozen in place as the blue creature raised itself and waddled slowly towards her."

I completed the story without touching my beer, absorbed by the simple but pure writing. Afterwards, I reached for my beer and noticed a pool of water had collected around its base. Carefully avoiding dripping over the manuscript, I took a huge gulp. Then I reread the story, which told a charming tale of the village of Santa Ana coping with the appearance of an unusual creature in its midst. After capturing the iguana, some townsfolk want to eat it, while others are convinced that it is a bad omen and must be released. The struggle between the town factions and the quiet majesty of the character Clara made compelling reading.

Perhaps too compelling. After my second reading, I doubted Humberto had written the story. I didn't know Humberto well, and while he was one of the most vocal students in the class, it was not clear how he could have authored such a touching — and profoundly wise — story.

I finished my beer and then walked onto the patio, still damp from the passing shower.

"What a strange little country," I thought.

Maria was waiting on the sidewalk, just as she had promised.

"Is this your home?" I asked as she got in the front seat.

"Perhaps," she said.

I laughed. "Maria, why are you so mysterious?"

She looked at me. "Why do you say that?"

"Well, you know," I said. "Instead of saying 'yes, that is my home,' or 'no, that is not my home,' you say 'perhaps.' That creates an air of mystery about you. I'm never sure what you mean."

"Ah," she said. "I understand. It is just my way," she said flicking her hand slightly to accentuate her point. "There is no mystery."

I laughed again and she flashed one of her extraordinary smiles.

We drove slowly through the eastern outskirts of Panama City toward the waterfront and the tourist section called Old Panama. Maria wore a white cotton blouse and a brightly colored skirt. Her hair was pulled back in a ponytail, and it blew about as the air from the open passenger window rushed past.

She gave directions and I parked when she gestured to an open parking space. I realized it was the same kind of take-charge gesture she made to Julio when she wanted him to take photographs. And like Julio, I simply did what I was told. Maria, it seemed, had that effect on men.

Old Panama is a series of stone ruins that sprawl over a large area facing the Pacific Ocean. Maria took her assignment seriously and was intent on telling me everything about the area's history.

"It is said that the pirate Henry Morgan was cruel and bloodthirsty," she said. "But that is not so. He did his work for the British government and attacked Spanish interests in the Americas. With many buccaneers, he landed on the Atlantic side and marched across to Panama City. He defeated a large Spanish force, then destroyed the city in January 1671. It is said that he burned everything and took the gold and silver. But it is unlikely he burned the city."

"Why is it unlikely?"

"The pirates only burned a city after they took the gold and silver," Maria said. "And sometimes they would hold the city as a ransom so that they would get more money. But Panama City burned before Morgan could do that. Perhaps the fire was an accident. Later he retreated to the Atlantic for his ships, but his buccaneers were very sad. They did not have as much gold and silver. Morgan took the gold and left most of his men behind."

"So these ruins are the ones he burned?"

"Yes, some are. But even when it was burned it was already an old city," she said. "It was first settled by Spain in 1519 by Pedro de Avila. It was the richest city in the Americas until it was burned."

We sat on a bench. The sky was bright blue with tufts of white clouds offering sporadic shade from the sun. The Pacific Ocean rushed the shore a quarter mile away. Tourists sauntered by. A light breeze skimmed off the ocean providing just enough relief from the heat and humidity to make the afternoon pleasant.

I tried to pay attention to the details of Maria's lecture on the early history of Panama but found myself looking at her face, observing a small mole on her left cheek I had not noticed before. The longer she talked the more I could observe her small, delicate wrists, strong calf muscles, long neck. She was quite beautiful.

"So," I said, trying now to break up the travelogue, "what did this Spaniard, Avila — was that his name? — want with Panama? Why did they settle here?"

"For conquest," she said. "It's always conquest, yes?"

"To conquer who?" I persisted.

"Avila needed a base to conquer the Incas in Peru," she said. "Panama was good for him. All the gold and precious stones were brought back here and counted. Then they were moved to the Atlantic side and shipped to Spain. For hundreds of years."

"You know," I said, "it's amazing that Spain was such a powerful country during that period. And now look at them."

"Ah, yes," she said. "But others take their place. It is always the same."

"Like the canal?" I said.

"Si, like the canal," she said steadily. "The Spaniards, the pirates, now the Americans. It is always the same for small countries like Panama."

"I wish it wasn't so, Maria," I said, turning to look at the warm Pacific.

We sat on the bench for a few moments, looking out over the morose stone ruins of Old Panama toward the surf of a stirred Pacific Ocean. I had no idea what Maria was thinking, but I was experiencing a unique emotion — a mixture of contentment and excitement. The scenery, cooling breeze, and sound of the ocean had a calming effect. But Maria created an electrical charge inside me that was both thrilling and distressing.

Seymour, my trusted advisor at Peary, pointed out that it's *always* acceptable to manipulate an asset with whatever tools I had at my disposal — money, drugs, friendship, and even sex. But it was *never* acceptable to fall for your asset.

"Are you listening to me, Haliday?" Seymour had said one day as we sat in the empty classroom. "It happens to nearly every field agent at one time or another. They meet someone who's instrumental to the mission. Maybe even vital to the mission. And they fall for them, head over heels. When that happens the mission's compromised, the agent is compromised. They can't act in the best interests of the mission, only the best interests of the person they've fallen for. Are you listening, Haliday?"

"Yes," I told him. "I got it."

"And don't forget the most obvious point: that *you* could be targeted by the person you've fallen for, who has flipped *you*! See," Seymour said, "we're back to rule Number One."

"Rule Number One," I said dutifully. "Trust no one."

"Just your station chief," he said. "Always your station chief; but no one else."

"What are you thinking of?" Maria said.

"Oh nothing," I said laughing. "Just daydreaming. You know it's beautiful here. Panama is a beautiful country. You're lucky."

"I'm sure America is beautiful," she said. "I have seen pictures."

"Have you been to the United States?"

"Oh no," she said, embarrassed at the suggestion. "Never. It is too far. Too expensive."

"I think you'd like the United States," I said. "There's plenty of opportunity there for everyone. And you are a bright woman. You would go far there."

"Please, Professor Baker," she said with a dismissive flick of her hand. "That is not possible. I am not so friendly to Americans."

"Well, you seem friendly to this American."

"You are my professor," she said quickly. "And we must go now."

She stood up, but I remained on the bench, squinting up at her as she loomed near the molten tropical sun.

"Only if you do me a favor," I said, suppressing Seymour's visage that lingered at the periphery.

"A favor?" she said warily. "I do not understand."

"Yes, a favor. Would you stop calling me 'Professor Baker?' My name is Nick."

I was surprised at her stern look. "You are my professor," she said. "It is not right to speak to you another way."

She stood looking at me and I smiled. It was a good smile on my part, really; kind of soft and vulnerable. Her scolding stance wavered a bit. She looked away, then back at me.

"We must go," she repeated.

"Do you promise?" I said, unmoving, my arms now spread out on the top of the bench back like a gliding albatross.

"No," she said looking away again. "Professor Baker you are making me—" she stopped and appeared to be sorting out the correct word, "—*nerviosa*, nervous. Please do not talk like this."

And only because I could see she genuinely was confused and upset, I stood up, and we walked silently back to the car.

Maria did not speak as we drove through the crowded streets of Panama. Many families were out on Sunday strolls, collecting in groups on street corners or in small parks for picnics.

"Maria," I said. "I'm sorry that I made you uncomfortable. I see that you're upset. Forgive me. I didn't mean any harm. You know, I really like your company. But I promise not to make you uncomfortable any more."

She looked at me sideways, squinting. She said nothing, which made *me* more uncomfortable. Don's face loomed in front of me, a scowling reminder of my mission.

"And don't forget Maria, that I've offered to help if you want any more photographs, or information — anything — really to help your group. I'm not sure we shouldn't just turn the canal over to Panama right now. It's absurd, really."

I could not tell whether she was pouting, angry, confused, or simply thinking. We just drove through the muggy afternoon in silence. I dropped her off, said good-bye and drove away. In my rearview mirror, I watched her. She stood on the sidewalk watching my car, then she turned slowly and started walking, her head up and her arms swishing the sides of her skirt in a determined stride.

CHAPTER 23

"Hey, is this Nick Baker?"

"Yes, it is," I said. "Who's this?"

"It's me, Fred Williams, over in Balboa. Elks Club. Remember?"

"Of course I do, Fred."

"Hey, some of the guys at the club wondered if you wanted to join us for a fishing trip and party at the Yacht Club?" he said, brimming with excitement. "You'll love it, Nick. Get you out of that pit over there and have some real American food."

It was not clear whether Don was behind the invite or not, but I was feeling so lonely that I jumped at the option. Fred gave me directions to get to the Yacht Club for the following Saturday.

Maria attended classes that week but barely acknowledged me after class. It became distressingly clear that my relationship with Maria had stumbled. She was the primary lead I had in my mission to penetrate leftist groups, but she was increasingly the object of my romantic attention. As a lonely undercover agent, lacking in both experience and confidence, I was desperate and lost.

At the end of one class I struck up a conversation with Humberto, my only other lead, but he seemed wary of me. I dreaded having to tell Don that I was at a dead end, so I started looking closely at the posters for the names of students. But no one was stupid enough to put their name on them.

And I noticed for the first time the occasional presence near the campus of members of the Panamanian National Guard. Outfitted in surplus US Army helmets and khakis, they walked in groups of four or more around the perimeter of the campus unarmed, sometimes flirting with coeds, but mostly behaving themselves. Nevertheless, there was palpable tension when they were present. You could see groups of male students giving them a wide berth.

Something must be happening at the government level. Perhaps President de la Guardia had been embarrassed by the size of the recent campus demonstration and was trying to clamp down on the youthful revolutionary zeal.

The Balboa Yacht Club was quite modest. It was nothing more than a concrete slab covered with a large, corrugated-metal awning. At its front stood a retaining wall overlooking a tiny beach that only showed itself at low tide. A pier of small wooden sailboats and powerboats stretched out on the side.

The club members were in full party mode by the time I showed up at 1 p.m. Fred found me right away and introduced me to a host of men and women club members. They were all tanned, very relaxed, and apparently having another wonderful day in this idyllic colonial outpost.

I did not see Don, so I hoped that he wasn't privy to my invite. I chatted with several couples. One of the men — Phil — was a canal pilot whose job was to drive a ship through the canal from end to end. He was brash, loud, and kept asking me about where I had gone to school in the states.

My cover school was the University of Maryland, and Phil was thrilled. It was his alma mater. Great, I thought. Just great. And sure enough, he peppered me with a million questions.

"Hey, did you ever take Western Civ from that old geezer, Jacobs?"

"No, sorry," I said.

"Well, you must have taken English Lit from Professor Jackson. Everyone took Jackson at one time or another, and you teach English Lit."

I could hear Seymour's voice clearly: "If someone insists on drilling into your cover, just shut up. And if that fails, just change the subject. Simple as that. Don't get trapped in a stupid lie by agreeing that you know such and such when it's clear you don't. Be brazen and move on to another subject. Being brash is better than being caught lying."

"So what years were you there again?" Phil asked.

"You know," I said, "let's talk about something else than college. Those days are gone. How about this great life you Americans have down here? You've got to admit, this is a pretty special place."

Phil's wife Nancy laughed and said, "It's our secret and you're not authorized to discuss it when you return to the states." That got a good laugh from the group and I slid away from them as soon as I could. Keeping cover with Panamanians was much less a problem than with this group of Americans.

"Hey there, Professor."

I turned to see Don holding two cans of ice-cold beer.

"Here you go, prof," he said loudly. "Get that taste of those crappy Panamanian beers out of your mind."

"Actually," I said taking the beer, "those beers aren't too bad at all."

He led me to the front of the club overlooking the pier and the grayish waters of the protective bay.

"Pretty nice view, huh?" he said.

"Very nice," I said smiling broadly with fake enthusiasm.

Don put his beer on the concrete ledge, grabbed a pack of Viceroys out of his top pocket, and lit one.

Blowing a long stream of smoke out through his nose and mouth at the same time, he said, "So, what's up?"

Quickly scanning to see who was nearby, I lied with more conviction than was warranted. "I'm making great progress. Getting closer to this group. It's just taking longer than I thought."

"Well, that's good news, Haliday. I was kind of worried about you over there. Wondered if this assignment was too much for you. But this is good news. Any idea on who the leaders are?"

"Negative," I said taking a swig of the beer. "They're still a tad leery of me. I'm an American, remember."

"A goddamn left-wing, beatnik, commie American," he said.

"Naturally."

"Well, keep me in the loop," he said. "I got Washington all over my ass. You have no idea what it's like to be in the field having your ass reamed from headquarters. They have no fucking idea what it takes to get things done down here. This ain't St. Louis or Minneapolis if you know what I mean."

"Boy, ain't that the truth," I said, feeling thankful that Don was dropping his guard with me.

"Oh, and another thing," I said taking a huge emboldened gulp of beer, "the courier who did a dead drop at the university saw me. Handed the envelope to me. Thought you should know."

"Assholes!" Don said. "When did this happen?"

I filled him in. Don shook his head.

"Complete incompetents," he said. "Goddamn it. I'll kill that son of a bitch."

"Well, get another courier," I said, thrilled that I could put Don on the defensive for once. "I don't want to be hanging out there with someone who can ID me."

"Assholes," Don said again.

By 4 p.m. the Yacht Club was very lively. It turned out that all the brave fishermen were too tipsy to attempt a fishing trip.

"We'll do it again," Fred said, unsteady on his feet. "No problem. We fish all the time. Lots of red snappers here. Great fish. Just a tad late in the day today, professor."

"Sure, Fred," I told him. "Don't worry about it. I'm having fun."

And that was the truth, although, like everyone else, I had one too many beers myself.

I said my good-byes and was starting to walk to my car when I heard someone calling my name. Turning I saw Nancy, the pilot's wife, waving me over to her. Walking back across the gravel parking lot, I smiled my best professor smile.

"Hi, it's Nancy, right?"

"Yes, it is. Boy, you have a good memory!" she gushed. "But of course, you're a professor."

It's funny, but I had never been in the presence of a woman who exuded so much raw sexuality as Nancy did that afternoon. Perhaps it was the alcohol she had consumed, or the alcohol I had consumed, or both. But standing next to her in the late-afternoon, Central American sun, I felt a 5,000-watt charge of sexual electricity.

What did she want? Why was she standing so close to me?

"So, Mr. Big Time Professor," she said, blowing cigarette smoke out of the corner of her mouth, "have you been able to tour the Canal Zone? Fred says you've been pretty busy over there with the natives."

She was flirting with me.

"Well, actually, Fred has been kind enough to show me the locks and a few other areas," I said carefully.

"I'd be glad to show you around the zone if you'd like," she said. "You know, a tour of our little corner of paradise. You'd be surprised how good life can be down here."

"Gee, Nancy, thanks for the offer," I said, quickly glancing around to see where her husband was. "I'll have to consider it."

She tilted her head and smiled, and then held out a piece of torn paper. "If you ever want a tour, just give me a call."

"Jeeze, thanks," I said. "I appreciate it."

She smiled and turned, walking back into the clubhouse. Getting into my car I could hear laughter as the club members got down to some serious work.

CHAPTER 24

Sunday morning I lay in bed, arm draped across my forehead, blocking out the light. It was cloudy outside, and I waited for the downpour to start.

The phone rang and I nearly knocked over the wind-up clock I had on my bedside table. Perversely, I expected to hear the sex pot Nancy offer to come over to show me around. And, as lonely as I was, it wouldn't be such a bad idea.

"Hello," I said.

"Professor Baker?"

"Yes?"

"It is Maria, Professor," she said. "Did I interrupt you?"

"No, Maria, not at all." I did not remember giving her my phone number and wondered groggily how she got it.

"How is your weekend?" she asked. Maria making idle chit chat on the phone with her English Lit professor? Something was up.

"Fine, so far," I said, sitting up in bed.

"Perhaps you would like to do sightseeing?" she asked. "Have you visited *la iglesia de San José?* The church with the golden altar? It is beautiful."

I felt a tinge of sadness for poor Maria. She was awkward and uncomfortable calling me that morning but was being a good soldier for someone, apparently. A proud and fierce young woman, she sounded lost trying to coax me out into the open on a cloudy Sunday morning.

"No, I have never seen the church," I said. "I've heard a lot about it."

"Would you like to meet me at the church? It is near the corner of *Avenida* A and *Calle* 8."

"Sure, what time?"

"Perhaps 1 p.m.?" she said.

"Great," I said. "See you there."

Seymour had many sayings he repeated to me in the hopes that his young charge wouldn't screw up his first assignment. One of his favorite sayings was, "If you suddenly have the feeling that you're being watched, then you're being watched. Don't over think it. Trust your instincts."

Of course, I had no instinct for field work, or so I thought. But sitting on a cement bench near the entrance of the Church of San Jose, I had the unmistakable impression that someone was watching me. It was an odd sensation — different from your run-of-the-mill paranoia. It was like being caught naked. I squirmed on the bench and had to keep reminding myself that this is exactly what I was here for. Maria had obviously let slip to someone in her group that this silly American professor had offered to help their cause. Presumably, the bait had been taken, and Maria, the reluctant tour guide, was being pressed into service. I was being evaluated from afar.

I saw her from about fifty yards. She had a short-sleeve, light-blue blouse and a long, ruffled skirt sporting alternating horizontal blue-and-white stripes. As happened more and more lately, part of my brain seemed perfectly focused on the mission at hand, while another, deeper part, was enthralled by Maria.

Beaming, I yelled, "Maria."

She saw me and smiled.

"Hello, Professor Baker," she said standing in front of me. "I'm so glad you wish to see the church. It is one of our most cherished treasures."

"Thanks for asking me," I said. "But you forgot something."

"I did?" she said nervously.

"Remember? No more 'Professor Baker.' It's 'Nick.'"

I don't know why I chose that moment to press her. It was a stupid trick, really. We were being watched, and I knew the last thing she wanted was to have any unpleasantness pass between us.

"Ah," she said annoyed. "That is correct. Yes. But it does not seem right to do so."

"Don't be silly," I said beaming. "Come on. You can say 'Nick,' can't you?"

"Perhaps," she said.

"Maria, are you always this serious?" I teased. "Remember, we're just a few years apart in age. We're sightseeing. This isn't the classroom."

"Very well," she said forcing a smile. "'Nick.' I have said it."

I held out my hand in a mock introduction. "Nice to meet you."

She held hers out and I grabbed it. It was small, delicate, and soft. She quickly pulled it from my grasp.

"Let us walk," she said.

The *Iglesia de San Jose* is a small, white-washed church with an ornate steeple housing an ancient bell. It's in a dense, old section of Panama with balconies overlooking narrow, colonial-era streets. It's a working neighborhood church, Maria said. We saw a black-frocked priest standing on the front steps talking to an older woman.

It was a warm, muggy afternoon and the sweat clung to the back of my shirt. Tiny beads of sweat collected on my forehead. Maria chatted away dutifully with her story about how a priest saved the gold altar of the church during Henry Morgan's famous pirate raid.

"The priest painted it black," Maria said. "When the pirate came he demanded to know what happened to the famous altar, but the priest said another pirate had taken it. The priest also convinced Henry Morgan to make a contribution to the church. He was a very brave and smart priest."

"But is the altar really solid gold?" I said.

"It is hand-carved wood that is covered in gold flake," she said.

She led me up the steps into the small, white-washed building. Inside the dimly lit church were rows of dark, wooden pews leading to an illuminated golden altar in the front. Maria genuflected and made a sign of the cross. I noticed that she had slipped on a thin white veil to cover her head. We walked up the aisle; she genuflected again and entered a pew. I followed. She kneeled, made the sign of the cross, prayed for a moment, and then sat back next to me.

"This is the famous altar," she whispered close to my ear. "Isn't it beautiful?"

"Yes," I said. An intricate and impossibly ornate gold altar stretched forty feet high. "How did anyone make something like this? It's so large."

"No one knows," she whispered, moving her head close to my ear again. "There is nothing like it in the world."

When Maria whispered it was the closest thing to physical intimacy we had. She would lean over and press against my shoulder lightly while tilting her head up and over to my ear. I could feel her warm breath on my neck, and it felt wonderful.

"Do you come here often?" I asked, making up questions to keep the moment going.

"No," she whispered. "This is not my church. It is too far. But I have attended two baptisms here. And one of my nieces was confirmed here."

"Are you very religious?" I asked.

"What do you mean?"

"Do you attend church every Sunday?"

"Of course."

"And confession?"

"Yes."

"Then you are very religious," I said.

"Yes, if that is what you mean by religious. Panama is a very Catholic country."

"With huge golden altars," I said.

"Yes," she said. "Tell me, professor," she said pulling away to look at my face, "are you making fun of my religion?"

"It's Nick, remember?"

"Nick, are you making fun?"

"No, of course not," I said. "I'm curious about Catholics that are so devoted."

Maria looked at me in a strange way and I instantly felt I had made a stupid mistake. She might see me as some infidel, a sinner to be shunned. It might not affect our professional relationship — the American spy trying to penetrate a leftist group — but it had great potential to disrupt the personal relationship I rashly was trying to foster.

"We should leave," she said suddenly, and we made our way out of the dark church into the gray light of clouds that pressed down like heavy, warm steel wool.

"So, that was interesting," I said, as Maria took her small veil off, folded it and put it in her purse. "What else can we do on this Sunday afternoon?"

"Let us walk," she said.

We passed a small park where there were several barbeques going and groups of families laughed and ate. I talked Maria into sitting on another bench.

She seemed more nervous now than in the church, and I guessed that our surreptitious observers were nearby. As we sat there, a perverse plot emerged from that self-serving and creative place in my brain.

What if I came across to Maria's handlers as unabashedly smitten by her? How would they react if they saw that Maria had some romantic hold over me? Wouldn't it dawn on them that Maria could leverage this "weakness" of the young American professor? If I was Maria's handler, that's what I'd do. It was a brilliant, utterly selfish plan and of course I embraced it.

"Maria," I said, "you seem nervous. Are you OK? Do you not feel well?"

"I am not nervous. Why do you say that?"

"I don't know, just an impression. Are you nervous to be seen with your professor?"

"No, of course not. Why would I be nervous? You are my professor. We are sightseeing."

I laughed and beamed a smile at her, looking and acting flirtatiously. "Tell me, Maria. Would you ever consider going out on a date with me? You know, to a movie, something like that?"

Maria snapped her head to look at me.

"A date?" she said. "What is a 'date'? I do not understand."

"You know," I said. "Go to a movie. Maybe go to dinner. Something like that."

"¿Una cita romántica?" she said, clearly startled.

"I don't know what you mean," I said laughing, "but from your expression, it seems like you understand."

She was plainly angry and gave me an icy stare that was hard to misinterpret.

"Gee," I said glumly. "I guess that's not such a good idea. Just thought I'd ask. You know Maria, I find you really interesting and I enjoy being around you. It would be fun to get to know you better. We're close in age. But I didn't want to offend you. I seem to be doing that a lot lately."

She looked out onto the small park. The clouds suddenly seemed closer and I wondered if we were about to get drenched. Watching her from the side, I noticed she was absently biting the inside of her lip.

We watched three young boys chase each other in a free-wheeling game of tag.

And then the rain came. It fell so quickly and hard that I had the sensation someone had just poured a pitcher of warm water on my head. Maria and I jumped off the bench while the families in the park collected their food and wares amidst peals of laughter.

We ran until we found a building awning and stood underneath with several other stranded strangers as the warm rain cascaded from the heavens.

"I'm soaked," I laughed. I could feel my shirt sticking to my skin and I pulled the cloth away from my chest.

Maria's hair was plastered onto her head in a funny way, and I noticed that her wet blouse was nearly transparent. I could see her bra strap on her shoulders and the thick white cups of her bra were clearly visible.

She tried to clean herself up, fluffing her hair and pulling her blouse away from her skin. She looked up at me and seemed embarrassed.

"Aiy," she said, shrugging her shoulders. "I feel so terrible. I am in such a mess."

"You look fine, Maria." But in truth, she looked lost and vulnerable. Her normal self-assurance was replaced by a schoolgirl's uncertainty.

CHAPTER 25

Two strange things happened after my next class.

First, Humberto approached me and timorously asked whether I'd had a chance to read his story.

"Yes," I told him. "It was an interesting story." He stood looking at me. I had concluded that he could not have written the story and decided wisely not to confront him.

"Did you like it?" he asked.

"Yes, very much."

"Do you think it could be made better?" he continued, trying to pry some reaction out of me.

"I don't think so," I said, pulling the manuscript out of my briefcase and handing it to him. "It's pretty well constructed as is."

"Oh," he said. "I see."

"Tell me, Humberto," I couldn't resist, "where did you get the idea to make the iguana the symbol of so much conflict in the town?"

"Ah yes," he brightened, reassured that I had at least read the story. "My *madre* told me the story."

"Your mother told you a story about a blue iguana?"

"Yes, she said it was a story in El Valle, the village where she lived. But I changed a few things, of course."

"Like what?" I pressed.

"Her story is about a coatimundi — you know the little animals in the jungle? She told me about a pure white coatimundi. But I felt guilty using the same animal. So I changed it."

"Is that all you changed?" I said.

"Well, of course, the mother in the story is my own mother," he said. "I hope I showed her dignity. Though, perhaps I was not so effective …" his voice trailed off.

"Humberto, your mother told you a story about a strange animal that comes to a mountain village, and you took that idea and fashioned your own story? Yes?"

Crestfallen, and misunderstanding my motive, Humberto said, "I'm sorry that it was not to your standard. Forgive me, Professor Baker."

"Humberto," I said, "don't you dare apologize! The story was excellent. I enjoyed it immensely. Your writing style is pure and unadorned. It really is quite unique."

"Unadorned?" Humberto said. "*No comprendo.*"

"Not flamboyant," I said. "Straightforward prose. Excellent work. Please continue to show me your writing. All of it."

"You will like to see more?" he said, grinning widely.

"Of course, but one story at a time!"

"Yes, most certainly. Thank you, Professor Baker. You are most kind." He shook my hand vigorously.

As I recovered from that surprise, another one approached.

"Did you ask Humberto if he was the rightful author?" Maria said.

"Yes," I said frowning. "He is indeed the author of record. And I feel foolish for doubting it."

Transitioning without a hitch, she said, "OK, perhaps we should go to a date."

"You mean 'go on a date'?" I said.

"Yes, that is what I mean."

"Gee," I said, "I'm thrilled. To be honest, Maria, I thought I offended you."

She flicked her hand dismissively. "I was not offended," she said. "Perhaps surprised. Yes, surprised."

We made innocuous chit chat, settling finally on dinner Friday evening. I said I'd pick her up in front of her house, but to my surprise, she told me I needed to meet her parents.

"It is necessary," she said frowning. "My mother, she will not be so happy."

"She doesn't approve of me?" I said. "Because I'm an American?"

"Perhaps," she said.

"And your father?"

"He is good," she said. "But he would like to meet you. It is necessary to meet my parents."

"Of course," I said.

I received another dead drop missive with the simple interrogative: "What are you doing?"

I sent back an equally truncated message: "Things are happening. Patience."

But I knew Don was not patient, and I received another dead drop ordering me to meet for lunch at the clubhouse again.

I had nearly finished my hamburger and was wondering if I had got the time wrong when he appeared.

"So, professor, how goes the battle? Things going well over there with the savages."

"Wish you'd stop referring to them that way, Don."

"Oh Christ, don't tell me you're going native on me," he said. "Don't dare pull that crap."

"I'm not pulling any crap on you, Don. I just don't think it's a great attitude to have about Panamanians."

"Now I'm worried about you," he said sitting down.

"Don't worry about me."

"So?" he said.

"Things are heating up," I said. "Looks like this girl —"

"Maria?"

"Yes, Maria. It looks like she's passed along my offer to someone because now she wants to spend more time with me. I think I was on display last Sunday. She took me sightseeing and I was being watched."

"How do you know? Did you spot anyone?"

"No, but I could just feel it. Maria was nervous. I could tell something was up."

"Well, this is good news indeed," Don said lighting up a cigarette. "I think you're onto something. Excellent. But you need to accelerate things."

"What do you mean?"

"We've got wind of a huge anti-American demonstration that's being planned. No details yet, but wondered if this Maria has said anything to you about it?"

"No. We don't really talk about that stuff — yet."

"Well, get on it, man," he said, blowing a stream of cigarette smoke toward me. "Time's a wasting."

"Don, if I press too hard it'll be obvious that I'm up to something. I can't take that chance."

"I'm telling you to take some chances, goddammit," he growled. "Get your ass in gear. You have no idea the kind of pressure that's coming from Washington to nip this canal thing in the bud. If I hear Suez brought up one more time I'm going to throw up. Thank god we've got other sources, or I'd really be up shit creek."

"What other sources?"

"Christ, Haliday, you think you're the only operative we've got in Panama? Hell, I'm running more locals than you could imagine. And spending a fortune doing it as well."

"Who are they? Do I know any of them?"

"Don't be stupid," he snorted. "I can't tell you that. You're all being run separately, and you know that's standard operating procedure. Can't have the entire operation compromised when a single agent goes down. Don't they teach you kids anything anymore?"

"Remember," I said defensively, "I was a rush job. You have to cut me some slack."

"Don't remind me," he said, sending a sarcastic stream of smoke shooting out of his pursed lips.

Standing, I said, "I'll keep you posted. And I'll try to move things along."

"Oh, and another thing," Don said, almost apologetically. "Here, this is for you." He reached into his shirt pocket and handed me a small sealed envelope. It had my name written in script on the front.

"What's this?"

"Just read it," he said.

I sat back down and tore it open. In longhand, it read: "Dear Nick, I'm going to be in town on Thursday night. I'll be staying at the Tivoli, room 810. Please stop by at 6 p.m. for dinner in my room. I'm told we cannot be seen in public for obvious reasons. Sincerely, Father."

When I looked up to speak, Don beat me to the punch. "It's not my idea of operating in the field, but I didn't have a choice. Why didn't you tell me your old man was so high up at State?"

"Well, I'm not going," I said, flipping the letter on the table. "That's absurd. I'm undercover for god's sake."

"Hey, keep your voice down," Don said. "And don't be an idiot. Of course you're going to see your old man, even if I have to drag you there myself."

"I'm not going," I said. "Don't even try to talk me into it."

"Wow," Don said eyeing me carefully. "I guess you and your old man don't get along very well."

"No, we don't."

"Can I give you some important advice?" Don said, leaning forward.

"I don't think I have a choice."

"Goddamn right you don't. Listen, if you don't show up, guess whose ass it is? Mine, not yours. Don't you dare stick me with this because I've got more important things to be doing than trying to explain to Washington why I couldn't set up a meeting between a high-ranking father and his son. You get my drift, Haliday. You will be there. Got that?"

I stared out the large windows onto the post office parking lot in front of the clubhouse.

"You're not answering me, Haliday. You on board with this request?"

"I got it," I said standing up to leave.

"Hey, take the letter," he said as I walked away, but I just kept going, out the door, down the steps into the heat and humidity that seemed more oppressive than normal.

The Tivoli was a grand old hotel straight out of a Rudyard Kipling novel of colonial India. It had a porch around the front circular entrance, with white wicker rocking chairs arrayed in groups on the wood-planked floor. Ceiling fans provided what breeze they could muster.

Something had happened to me since I read the letter Don gave me. Thoughts of my mother's death kept colliding with my loneliness and longing for family. I still harbored a smoldering anger at my father for fostering the nomadic lifestyle that seemed to damage my mother.

Yet, oddly, my mother's image had grown tarnished. She had not been well for many years. I had trouble conjuring up the pleasant family memories of her, just the excruciatingly embarrassing ones of her being drunk.

My father, on the other hand, was never drunk. He never hit me or did anything that demeaned me. His crime, in my muddled thinking, was *absence*. He wasn't there physically or emotionally for me. He couldn't save me from the disappointments of seeking friends in new schools, or the struggles with bullies who seemed to sniff out new students like me.

And he couldn't save me from the countless episodes of attending to a drunken, helpless mother.

I guess I didn't hate my father, but did I love him? And did I really love my mother, the woman who tormented me?

Maybe I just didn't have a lot of practice at love; just a well-developed expertise at self-protection from emotional pain.

But a crack had opened in that thick protective shell. Her name was Maria. I was beginning to care about her. I wanted her to think about me and care about me. How strange it felt to *really* want someone to care for me.

By the time I got to room 810 and knocked twice, I was not the old Nick, but not quite the new one either.

The door opened and there stood my father, beaming.

"Nick," he said reaching out and embracing me.

"How are you?"

"OK, I guess."

He had dinner for two set at a small table and I could smell the aroma of grilled steak.

"Would you like a drink before dinner?" he asked. "Beer, Scotch?"

"Um, sure. A beer would be nice."

"OK," he said, opening a bottle of Schlitz and pouring it into a tall, V-shaped pilsner glass, very much in style those days. We sat down and my father chatted on. He carefully avoided asking me a direct question about my work.

"You know," he said, cutting his steak, "this canal situation is worrying the administration no end. Lots of jabbering coming from the hawks at Defense and even your folks at the Agency seem to be more aggressive. Alas, we timid little Staties are recommending a more conciliatory approach. Less brawn, more brains kind of thing. But I think we're losing that battle."

My father was clever to discuss the canal because I was very curious.

"What does 'more aggressive' mean?" I said, toying with my steak.

"You know, bring in the big guns. Wine?" he asked raising the bottle in the center of the table.

I shook my head.

"So, what is State recommending?" I asked.

"Oh, the usual sensible approach: dialogue, discussion, probably mild concessions. Stuff like that. Our antiquated view is that some of these problem areas around the globe are actually sincere nationalistic outpourings masquerading as Marxist rebellions, usually aided and abetted by Red agitators. But we think the best way to defuse these pressure points is to acknowledge the problem and make some concessions. I mean, the colonial era is over."

"And what's the agency's view?" I asked.

"Oh, that view is easy: 'Off with their heads,'" he said raising his steak knife and making a horizontal swipe.

"So, Nick, how are things going for you down here? Are you doing well? Do you like your work?"

"Yeah," I replied. "It's interesting, but also confusing at times. I can't go into it deeply, for obvious reasons. I was rushed into this assignment so it's all new to me. But I like the challenge."

"I hate to ask this, Nick," he said putting down his fork and knife and holding his glass of red wine with two hands, "but are you safe? Are you in danger?"

I laughed, though it might have been a nervous laugh. "Why do you ask?"

"Just what we've heard through the grapevine."

"Can you be more specific?"

"The Pentagon considers the canal a vital national interest and is pulling out all the stops to tamp down Panamanian agitation. Unfortunately, we hear the Soviets are also treating this with equal intensity.

There's talk of Eastern Bloc agents doing the heavy lifting, and some of those folks are notoriously violent."

"That's interesting," I said. "I can attest to the fact that things are heating up. I feel it every day. My boss is frothing at the mouth."

"Do you feel safe?" he persisted.

"Yes. Well, mostly. Like I said, this work is new to me. But they prepared me well and I feel confident I can help the cause, whatever that is."

My father smiled. "That's a healthy sign of cynicism. You know I'm not a fan of the agency and some of its methods, but, well, we do need folks to do the hard, dirty work every now and then."

"It does feel like dirty work."

We ate in silence. Then after a few minutes, he put down his knife and fork.

"Nick, I was hoping that over time you would soften a bit toward me. That you would forgive me for the things you think I did to you and your mother."

He caught me completely off guard, and my fork froze halfway to my mouth with a triangle of steak on it.

"What do you mean?" I stammered.

"You know what I mean, Nick. Maybe I wasn't the best father. I know I wasn't there for you and your mother. I might have been blind to how your mother was. Perhaps I couldn't deal with the reality that she was sick. That's my fault and I'll live with that the rest of my life. I can accept that. But here's my question — when are you going to forgive me?"

I looked up because I could hear his voice crack. The pain on his face startled me and I felt ashamed that I brought my father to the brink of tears.

He looked down at his food and choked back his anguish. I was stunned at the emotional intensity of his feelings — and my own throttled emotions.

"Nick," he said, his voice wavering, "there's only the two of us left in this family. We have so much to live for, to enjoy together. Don't you think something like forgiveness is in order? If not forgiveness, how about civility? Your disdain for me is so upsetting. I'm utterly depressed about it."

If you spend your life weaving a thick, concrete cocoon around yourself it doesn't come crashing down in one fell swoop. But it does crack.

"I … Father. I don't know what to say. I'm having troubling thinking right now. You're right. This is the family that's left: just you and me. I suppose I haven't been the best son. I could have helped Mother more. Maybe if I had—"

"Don't say that, Nick," he said with sudden ferocity. "You were a child for god's sake. I was the other adult. It was my responsibility to help Margaret, not you. It's me that made all the mistakes. I tried to talk her into a sanitorium, but she was adamant about not leaving you alone."

Flustered and confused, I stood up.

"Father, I feel very strange right now. I'm sorry. I think I have to leave."

"But we haven't finished dinner."

"I know. It's a great dinner and I'm really glad you visited me. I'm kind of cut off from everyone and everything I'm familiar with, and right now, I feel like I need to clear my head. Good night," I said, putting the napkin onto my seat.

He walked me to the door and said nothing, though his eyes were watering. He gave me a powerful hug, then said, "Please be safe, Nick. I miss you and don't want anything bad to happen to you. This is a place where bad things happen. I can't let more bad things happen to my family. I just can't."

"I'm going to be fine, Father. But thanks for your concern. It means a lot to me. I know I have trouble showing it, but I'm glad you visited me."

I walked out of the room, into the hallway, and through the lobby in a complete trance.

CHAPTER 26

Maybe I had been depressed all my life and just didn't know it. I would sometimes have these days when I would turn sour. In Panama, it had happened a couple of times. I would sit in my apartment all day and read a book, drink beer, and just grow weary. If it was raining, I would stand at the slider with my arm against the frame, and just watch the warm sky melt into the saturated ground.

The day after I left my father sitting at the dinner table, I was in one of those moods. It was a Friday and I had no classes. I was supposed to see Maria that evening for our dinner date and I wanted to cancel it. I was not up to balancing the demands of my job — to get access to Maria's group of leftists, with the demands of my psyche — to get access to Maria's affection.

Only as an afterthought did it occur to me that I didn't have Maria's phone number. How was I going to cancel the dinner?

I went for a walk and felt better instantly. The vision of my father left standing there in the doorway was haunting me. He seemed so painfully alone. In fact, he was alone like me. Maybe even depressed and alone like me.

By the time I was to pick up Maria, I felt much better. Seeing her would certainly brighten my day, though it also created complications that I was struggling with. Was Maria *really* doing the bidding of some leftist organization? I told Don I was convinced of it, but was I really? It was certainly possible that Maria was exactly who she presented herself as: a college student resisting the awkward flirtations of her professor. This could be a classic wild goose chase and Don would explode if it turned out that way.

And of course, there was the obverse: What if Maria was exactly who I thought she was? A lower-level functionary in a leftist student organization who had presented her leadership with a prize of sorts: an innocent, left-leaning American professor to be used by them at their whim. My attachment to Maria complicated everything. Seymour was right but it was too late. "Your mark is your mark," he had told me. "They are not your girlfriend, boyfriend, best friend, or even a real friend. Don't *ever* screw that one up."

"Hello," she said, putting on her best strained smile. "Please come in. My parents are looking forward to meeting you."

She lived in a large rambling, ranch-style home in a solid upper-class neighborhood of Panama City. We entered into a foyer covered with large glazed terra cotta tiles. She led me down a hallway into a large well-appointed living room. I was dreading the entire awkward parent thing.

As we walked in, her parents were talking animatedly. They both rose and stopped talking.

"Mr. Santiago," I said trying to take the lead, "pleased to meet you." He stepped forward, smiling grandly. He enveloped my right hand with both his hands.

"So you are the American professor!" he said in perfect English. "It is good to meet you finally."

Maria walked over to stand next to her mother. "Professor Baker, this is my mother."

I took several steps toward her and held out my hand. Mrs. Santiago was not happy, and it took what seemed like every ounce of energy to extend her hand. And I can certify that it felt like a dead catfish. She pulled the corners of her lips back just enough to expose her teeth. The effect was not unlike an aging barracuda circling the reef for easy prey.

"Please sit down," her father said, gesturing to the couch. Maria sat down at the other end of the couch.

"So, tell me, Professor, how is your stay in Panama going? Are you enjoying our small country?"

"It's been a wonderful stay so far," I said. "I love it here. Though, I had no idea that the rainy season was this rainy. We don't have rain like this where I'm from."

This generated the appropriate level of polite laughter.

"And where are you from, exactly," he asked.

I stuck to the cover in minute detail and was proud of myself at the end. I had almost convinced myself I had grown up in Wisconsin and attended the University of Maryland.

Maria would often translate some of my sentences in Spanish, so I gathered the Iron Maiden mother was not as fluent as her dad.

After almost thirty minutes of this, Maria stood up and said that we should go. I couldn't wait to evacuate and suffered the dead-catfish handshake from Mom and the double-handed one from Dad.

In the car, Maria said, "My father really likes you. I can tell."

"He seems like a really nice guy. And your mother was very cool. I just loved her."

Maria shot me a sideways glance and then smiled. "You are being funny."

"Yes," I laughed. "I am. Thank heavens you warned me. I'm glad there were no handguns lying about. We might not be going to dinner tonight."

Maria laughed so heartily that I was startled. She dropped her head back against the seat top and let go with a howl. Watching her from the side, I was again struck by her delicate beauty.

"Sometimes you are very funny, Nick," she said. The fact that she called me Nick without prompting was not lost on me.

The restaurant was fancy and only a couple of blocks from the Hilton. Maria had recommended it. She looked terrific in a sleeveless print dress that fell to her knees. As silly as it sounds, I had never seen her in a sleeveless top and the full effect of her slightly muscular arms was enthralling.

And yet, as the dinner wore on, I felt the sluggishness that had consumed me earlier in the day begin to resurrect itself. I grew less talkative and more self-absorbed. It happened so gradually that I didn't notice.

But Maria did.

"Nick," she said. "You do not enjoy your meal?"

"No, this snapper is excellent. Why do you ask?"

"Oh, I thought you were not enjoying it. You seem disappointed. I was not sure."

"No, it's fine," I said.

"You seem different," she said. "Is something wrong?"

"No. Nothing's wrong. Really."

"I was worried that I was disappointing you," she said, her eyes dropping. "I'm just a student. And you are a distinguished professor. Perhaps my conversation is not what you are used to."

"Good grief, Maria. You couldn't be more wrong. I enjoy our time together. In fact, to be perfectly honest, the best times I've had in Panama were spent with you. Honestly."

She brightened noticeably, and then, in her blunt style that I was still not used to, she said, "May I ask a personal question?"

"Sure."

"Why are you so sad sometimes? Tonight you seem sad."

"I do?"

"Yes. I thought maybe you were unhappy with me."

I sighed and looked away absently to a nearby table of two couples who were loudly enjoying themselves.

"I think it's family issues that are bothering me, Maria," I said looking back at her. "I have these family things that just won't go away. I wish they would. But they won't. It has nothing to do with you. I should learn how to put them away."

"Is it about your parents? Your brother or sister? Do they make you unhappy?"

"Well, my mother is dead, and I have no brothers and sisters."

"I'm sorry," she said quickly. "Please forgive me. I do not wish to pry."

"No, it's OK. It's just me. Me and my father."

"Are you close to your father?" she asked.

"No, far from it. Not close at all."

"Oh, I see," she said. "Do you wish to be closer to him?"

"I guess so."

"Mmm," is all she said.

We drove around the city after dinner and Maria pointed out some of the landmarks, including the ornate embassies and the presidential palace. I had started to lighten up as Maria took pains to draw me out. I deeply appreciated her doing that.

But almost as an afterthought I remembered what the hell I was doing in Panama in the first place. I felt guilty and conflicted for proceeding, but I felt Don's visage staring down on me.

I threw out a piece of bait — a huge chunk of Red meat that no self-respecting leftist, nationalist agitator could avoid.

"You know, this is such a beautiful country," I said. "It's almost criminal that you're not able to have access to all its assets."

"¿Qué quieres decir? I am sorry — what do you mean?" she said.

"The canal, Maria. It's ridiculous that Panamanians are not allowed to run the canal. It's just another example of colonialism at its worst."

"Yes," she said looking out the side window at the black Pacific Ocean as we sped by. "It is tragic."

"And Maria, you don't have to trick me as you did before to get my participation with your group. It's a just cause and I'd be proud to help."

I could feel her looking at me for a long time and wondered whether I had been too ham-handed. I had no choice. If Maria was going to give me entry into her organization, I needed to find out soon.

And of course, in my naïve and self-centered thinking, I was hoping that Maria and I could carry on our awkward courtship without the encumbrances of the whole spy-counterspy thing.

CHAPTER 27

The following Tuesday was interesting, in a painful way.

After class, Maria lingered, and we walked down the hall together. I was lugging a pile of papers that needed correcting, and the thought of spending the next several days grading them was daunting.

And of course, I was waiting to see whether Maria was going to allow me to help her group. It needed to happen soon.

Don had sent a dead-drop note confirming a demonstration was in the works and asked if I had anything to report.

"Soon," was my reply.

My gambit with Maria was to bring up the demonstration. I would offer to attend with her. It would be a sign of my political leanings and enthusiasm.

But the situation was complicated, of course. In retrospect, I think we were falling in love, but I was so confused about everything in my life that I could only recognize a slight increase in the intensity of our relationship.

That Tuesday Maria and I parted after class and I went to the library. I didn't feel like going back to my apartment to spend the next several days entombed with thirty-two papers on "The Tragic Nature of F. Scott Fitzgerald."

At around 5 p.m. I collected my papers and sauntered out to the parking lot. It was a normal, oppressively humid day. The sun was still high enough to be a bother, and I was afraid my sweat was going to stain some of the papers at the bottom of the stack I was lugging.

Arriving at the car, I put down my brief case and — holding the stack in my left arm — I fished for my keys in my pants pocket.

"Gringo," someone said from behind.

I turned to see three young men looking at me. The one in the middle wore a plaid shirt and had a baseball bat in his right hand. Both his partners wore white cotton t-shirts and shorts.

"Yes?" I said.

They walked toward me slowly. The one in the middle wore a huge grin, but his pals were much grimmer.

"*¿Qué pasa?*" I asked.

For a trained CIA field operative I was woefully slow on the up-take. The smiling one stepped forward and simultaneously jammed the fat end of the bat into the fleshy area above my belt. It sent a nauseous wave of pain through my body. I doubled over reflexively and felt the weight of the bat come down on the back of my neck.

I landed hard on my knees, and for some reason known only to teachers of the world, I refused to let go of the pile of papers cupped against my body by my left arm.

I was surprised by the sound of a crunch when a sneaker caught the side of my nose.

There were too many kicks to count, one of them catching me on my cheekbone and another one landing squarely on the pile of buffer-ing school papers. This seemed to enrage the attackers and one of them followed with a well-aimed kick at my exposed rib cage.

While they did their manly work, I tried to scoot my body under-neath the car, but I could only get my head behind the driver's side wheel well. I balled up the best I could and even used the F. Scott Fitz-gerald papers as a shield against my face.

If my head was now protected, my stupid ass was decidedly not. One of the three musketeers got behind me and let fly with a kick, the toe of his sneaker catching my testicles square on.

I thought I was going to die.

I slumped forward and finally — forgive me, educators everywhere — let go of the Fitzgerald papers.

This must have alarmed my attackers because the only thing they did afterwards was to give me a single half-hearted kick in my butt. Then one of them laughed. With my right cheekbone planted squarely on the pavement under the wheel well, I could see their feet skittering away and heard them laughing hysterically.

I was saved from feeling utter humiliation by the pain that kept me occupied.

Someone tapped my exposed left arm urgently.

"Señor, señor," the person said. "¿Se encuentra bien?"

I slowly extracted myself from under the car, feeling more and more pain in the ribs. I thought I was going to throw up but fought the urge. I finally righted myself, planting my sore butt gingerly on the ground with my back against the car.

Two people leaned over me. As soon as they saw my face, they both pulled back in alarm.

"Aiy," one of them said, grimacing.

They kept speaking to me in Spanish and I kept repeating "No hablo español." I tried to stand up but faltered.

I finally forced myself up, wobbled for a second like a newborn giraffe, then leaned against the car. I noticed the pile of Fitzgerald papers on the ground and pointed to them. "Por favor?" I said huskily.

One of the men bent down and collected them for me. I slowly unlocked the car, then put my briefcase in along with the Fitzgerald papers. I waved off my saviors and started the car, backing out slowly. I could see that a crowd had gathered, and they watched as I drove slowly away.

I purposely did not look at myself in the rearview mirror.

Who were those thugs? Students? I couldn't place any of them, though maybe I had seen the smiling one before. They didn't rob me, that's for sure. Leftists on the hunt for Americans? Maybe it was a warning. What were they warning me about?

Now on full alert, I parked close to the stairwell leading into the apartment complex. Making sure I was alone, I painfully made it out of the car, grabbing all my stuff. I had a feeling that at least one of my ribs was broken or cracked. I was having trouble breathing. And my face felt numb. Vainly, I wondered how disfigured I was.

Inside the apartment, I dropped everything on the couch and made it to the kitchen. Taking the ice tray out, I emptied it into a small towel and brought it gingerly to my left cheekbone.

I went into the bedroom, kneeled in front of the dresser and pried away the bottom molding. Reaching in I pulled out my pistol and stuck it in the top of my pants in the back, draping my pulled-out shirt over the handle.

I had no idea what was happening. I was feeling threatened and really scared for the first time in my life. While I knew intellectually this business was supposed to be dangerous, there's nothing like having someone score a triple off the back of your neck to make it all real.

It was time for an inspection, and holding the ice against the left side of my face, I went into the bathroom and looked, slowly pulling the cloth away.

What a mess! I had a deep contusion below my left eye that was red and purple. And my nostrils sported coagulated blood dripping in two neat vertical stripes, like a bad parody of Adolph Hitler.

Before I could clean my wounds, or even feel deeply sorry for myself, the front door shook with an urgent knock. It was followed by more pounding.

I tiptoed to the front door and put my eye against the peephole. In perfect fish-eye distortion, I could make out the worried visage of Mr.

Delgado from the university, as well as two stern-faced, portly members of the local constabulary.

Delgado brought his hand up to his mouth in alarm after he saw me. One of the cops grimaced.

Delgado, in between profound and repetitive apologies, translated to the police the details of my attack. We went over it several times until I couldn't stand it any longer and told Delgado I needed to rest.

The police said they were going to station someone at my front door permanently and I told them it was not necessary. It would be too much fuss for the neighborhood, I said. Besides, I told Delgado, it was clear to me that if they had wanted to kill me they would have.

The cops nodded in agreement when Delgado translated. Nevertheless, they said, they were going to detail a car to the neighborhood.

Delgado told me that Dr. Rodriguez was beside himself in horror at the attack and wanted to make sure that I knew they were going to do everything they could to bring the attackers to justice.

I finally pushed him and the cops out the door right after the sun had set. They were no sooner down the stairwell when the phone rang. It was Dr. Rodriguez and he commenced to apologize with such profundity that even I started feeling sorry for the guy who just got his ass whipped. Dr. Rodriguez must have gone on for twenty minutes, and to be honest, I was moved by his concern.

Exhausted and very, very sore, I considered visiting the emergency room of the local hospital. After hanging up the phone, I grabbed a beer and sat down on the couch. The pistol stabbed into my back, so I pulled it out and jammed it under the center cushion.

Taking a deep breath, I tried to calm myself by closing my eyes and leaning back.

There was another loud and urgent knock at the door.

"Christ," I said standing up. I took a step toward the door, but stopped and went back for the gun, jamming it behind my belt at the back and covering the handle again with my shirt.

Looking through the peephole I had trouble seeing in the darkness. Then my visitor stood underneath the light and I quickly opened the door.

"Oh!" Maria said, covering her mouth with her hand. I turned and made my way back to the couch and flopped down. She closed the door and followed me, standing above me.

I closed my eyes and held the ice pack to my face.

"Maria, I swear to god I cannot answer the door or the phone any more today. I need to rest. I'm so damn sore."

I opened my eyes to find her gone. Then I heard rustling in the kitchen. She came back after a few minutes with a small bowl of warm water and a facecloth. Sitting next to me she proceeded to dab and clean.

She didn't ask what happened or how I felt. She simply cleaned me up little by little, sometimes making a "tsk, tsk" sound and shaking her head. At other times she simply sighed. That was it.

It was fair to say I was feeling disoriented and a tad reckless. I could feel Maria's face next to mine as I leaned back with my eyes closed, being swabbed. Sometimes her warm breath cascaded down my face and neck. I could almost taste her.

Finally, she sat back and said, "I think you are clean now."

Opening my eyes, but with my head back staring at the ceiling, I said, "No. You missed this," pointing to a spot at my hairline. She got up and stooped over me. Only inches separated our faces. When she couldn't find the mark, her eyes shifted to mine.

She remained still and I slowly raised myself the few inches and gently kissed her. She stopped breathing and pressed back slightly.

Swoon is perhaps too strong a word to describe my reaction, especially for a man in my weakened condition. But my chest and stomach swarmed with electrical energy and I wanted more.

Maria stood up slowly and wagged a finger at me. "No *más*," she said.

"Great," I said. "Deny a dying man his last request."

"I am so sorry what happened to you today," she said. "It is really bad. I cannot believe it."

"Neither can I," I said. "Jumped by three thugs. Felt like a complete idiot."

"They were not criminals," she said.

"Well, in my country assault is a crime. That makes them criminals."

"But they are not criminals."

"Well, if not criminals, what would you call them?"

"Stupid young men," she said. "And jealous. Men are so jealous. I cannot understand why they must fight."

"Jealous?" I said.

"Yes. Jealous. It was my boyfriend who did this to you," she said. "And his two brothers. Reynaldo and Franco."

CHAPTER 28

"I didn't even know you had a boyfriend!"

"You are shouting," she said.

"I am?"

"Yes. You should be calm."

"How can I be calm? I was almost killed today."

She made a give-me-a-break look.

"And when were you going to tell me about this killer boyfriend of yours? And his psychotic brothers, Pedro and Poncho."

"Reynaldo and Franco," she corrected.

"Jeeze," I said, shaking my head. "You should tell him to quit beating up people. It's not nice. And it hurts. Look at me."

"Oh, you are not so bad," she said.

"And it sounds like you're defending him."

"No!" she said. "That is not true. He is not my boyfriend any longer."

"Mmm," I said. "Well, just as well. He's in big trouble. Dr. Rodriguez just called me. They're going to find him and his pals."

She took a step closer and pointed a fierce finger at me. "You will not tell about him," she said. "You must promise. He will be in big trouble."

"You must be kidding, Maria! Just look at my face. I most certainly will tell on him. And his crazy brothers."

You could say that she gave me a very bad — no, extremely menacing — look, but that would be understating it. Putting both hands on her hips she glared. "You must promise, Nick. You will not tell. Yes?"

"Jeeze, Maria, is everyone like this down here?"

"You must promise," she repeated, her face tightening at the corners.

"No, Maria. They're criminals!"

"You are not so funny, Nick. Promise."

I was not sure who was worse, Maria or her boyfriend. I sighed deeply and let my head fall back again. The weight of this day was pulling me down.

"On one condition," I said finally.

"What is this 'condition?' What does that mean?" she said carefully.

"I won't say anything if you give me one more kiss. Just one."

Maria dropped her hands from her hips and crossed them in front of her chest, like a disgusted parent. She stared at me. I stared at her.

"Just one," she said finally.

"Only one. That's all," I lied.

After a moment she took the several steps toward me, leaned forward slowly and braced her hands at the top of the couch on either side of my tilted-back head. Lowering her face, she kissed me hard. And then she parted her lips slightly and with her teeth, she delicately gripped my bottom lip and tugged it ever so slightly.

Even my wounded loins swarmed with extraordinary sensations.

She stood upright, looking down on me for a second, sighed, then turned toward the door.

"Hey," I said hoarsely. "One more."

She wagged a finger at me. "No."

"I'll call Dr. Rodriguez and tell him about your boyfriend," I said lamely.

"You would not dare," she said opening the door.

She was right. I would not dare. Not now.

I hadn't the faintest idea what I was doing with Maria.

I could justify this breach of field protocol by saying I was rushed into action without proper training, that I was too young. And I was a virgin. And lonely. And probably even depressed and vulnerable.

But none of it mattered. I was smitten like a gooey-eyed, slobbering idiot. I could not stop thinking of her. I wondered endlessly whether she was a virgin. Maybe that's why she went to confession. Maybe not. And how could she date that thug — the maniac with the Louisville Slugger?

I was too mixed up to care.

But Don kept me on track. He demanded to see me two days later. We met at a gravel parking lot overlooking the American-built causeway at Fort Amador in the Canal Zone. It was our emergency meeting site and Don wanted me familiar with it.

I anticipated that as soon as he saw me, he'd be all over me with a million questions about my facial injuries. I had a pretty good cover story about being jumped by a bunch of anti-American terrorists, leaving the psychotic boyfriend part out.

Don was leaning on the hood of his car, looking out into the Pacific Ocean when I pulled up to the overlook. I could see smoke rising above him as he tore through another of his cigarettes.

When he saw me, he laughed so hard I thought he was going to fall into the Pacific.

"Woo, wee, Haliday, the things we have to do for our country! God, look at you!"

And before I could start relaying my heroic struggle with the forces of evil, he said, "And of all people, her goddamn boyfriend. And his brothers! God, that's funny." He slapped his knee. Several times.

"Well," he said gathering himself, "no one's gonna say you didn't hold your cover. You're busy playing the love-struck American professor

— sweet talking that little Chiquita — and you get clobbered by her boyfriend. Well, at least you've got her attention now. She'll do anything for you, her shining knight."

He laughed so hard this time that he started coughing.

"How in the hell did you find that out?" I said.

"Oh god, Haliday, we're running so many lines in there right now you're all stepping over each other."

"Well, it's reassuring that I'm being watched," I said. "You could have told me."

I leaned on the front of his car and both of us looked out into the turbulent bay. A steady wind was up, pushing small white caps in horizontal bands toward the huge stones at the base of the causeway.

"You're not being watched, Haliday," he said, absently trying to remove a piece of tobacco from his lip. "Why the hell would we do that?"

"Just seems like you know everything that's going on."

"Wish I did," he said. "Which reminds me Romeo, have you gotten anything from that girl on the demonstration that's coming up?"

"Nope."

"Well, get something, will ya! We're running out of time and I can't figure out what they're going to do. What the hell good are you if you can't even get the simplest things out of these people?"

It still amazed me how quickly Don could go from laughter to rage. It was unnerving.

"I'll find out," I said brazenly, staring out to sea.

"Good," he said. "You do that. And quickly."

We sat together quietly for a moment, then I stood up off the hood. "I'll see ya," I said.

"Yep," Don replied, sucking on his cigarette, the wind whipping the exhaled smoke backwards like a contrail on a jet.

I drove away, and looking in my rearview mirror, I could see him motionless, staring out into the frothy sea.

★

I attended my next class, proud that I'd graded all my Fitzgerald papers. One of them was slightly torn, and another had a huge scuff from the shod foot of one of my bat-swinging attackers.

It was awkward standing in front of the class because they were whispering and pointing at the various facial marks from my gallant struggle. Before I could start, Hector, one of my most talkative students, stood up and pronounced, for the entire class, that they were sorry and ashamed about what happened to me.

"Please do not feel badly about Panamanians," he said. "We are not all like those animals who did this to you. We are happy to have you as our teacher and have learned a great deal about literature." At that, the class started clapping.

I was caught off guard by the speech and felt a sudden rush of emotion. Then I quieted everyone down.

"Hector, don't worry about my feelings for Panama. It is a grand country of fine, proud people. I feel bad, sometimes, about how we Americans treat you and, in fact, I am ashamed. But, like Panama, I am strong. Thank you for your concern."

After class, several groups stayed behind to chat. Maria lingered.

CHAPTER 29

"You are making me angry," she said. "Why do you talk like this in the class?"

"Talk like what?"

"Your anti-American statements. This is not your concern. You keep saying it to the students. What are you trying to do?"

"Maria, I think my political opinions are pretty well known. And the longer I'm here — except when I'm getting beaten up by jealous boyfriends — the more I like this country. And its people. Especially the women." I smiled.

She looked at me, looked away, then looked back into my eyes. Her demeanor was softer, and she looked spent. She sighed.

If I could have figured out a way to kiss her then and there, I would have, but that would not work.

"Do you think the other students know about us?" I said.

"What do you mean?" she said, her face twisted in alarm.

"You know," I said.

"I do not know," she said. "What are you talking about?"

"That you're in love with me."

She rolled her eyes, shook her head, and made a small sideways step, putting one hand on her hip.

"You are impossible, Nick. Are you always so impossible? Are you like that to your American girlfriends, Nick?" She was mocking me in that flirtatious, aggressive Maria-kind-of -way. When provoked, her small nose flared, and she made short, compact physical gestures, like a flick of the wrist, or a twist of her neck that sent her hair flying just so.

And it was at this moment that I also suspected Maria was not a hardened member of a communist cell with access to higher-ups but was probably a low-level functionary. Someone who held posters. Or took photographs. An attractive and strong-willed poster holder, but still, in the end, a simple poster holder who knew no one important and was useless to someone like Don.

Or that was my hope, anyway.

"Sometimes we just guess wrong," Seymour told me one afternoon, drinking Cokes in the empty cafeteria. "We may have the wrong instinct or the wrong intel. Just move on. Don't look back. Don't take it personally. It's not a perfect science. Just avoid fatal mistakes. The big ones. We're spies, not gods."

"OK," Maria said. "If you wish to go to a demonstration, I will take you. I will let you know when there is one. I will look out for you. Perhaps one day when you are a famous American novelist you will write about our victorious rebellion."

"You sound like Karl Marx," I said laughing. "I like Maria better."

Then Maria dropped her guard and for just a moment looked at me with a sad, vulnerable face. I had only seen this Maria a couple of times and it was very disarming.

"You are making me nervous," she said softly, looking absently at the top button on my shirt. "Why are you doing this? You should leave me alone. You do not understand the situation."

"Too late," I said.

Maria and I sat in a tiny restaurant near the university, eating empanadas and drinking Coke. The farther we were from the school, the more relaxed and self-confident she became.

Our relationship had settled into that complicated netherworld between verbal flirtation and teasing physicality. Maria, for instance, would tolerate me touching her arm or grabbing her wrist to make a point, but would not allow me to put my arm around her. We kissed several times, and while they lasted, the kisses were passionate and left me breathless.

The sexual tension heated many of our interactions like a low-grade fever. Interestingly, I dropped my guard with Maria about my family.

"So out of the blue, I just told my father," I said. "I could tell he was surprised to hear from me."

"Did you tell him you missed him?" she asked.

"It was awkward, but yes, I did tell him."

"Was he happy?"

"Yes, extremely."

"How did you feel?"

"I felt good. I mean it was intense, but I felt good. And relieved."

"You are a strong man to do that," Maria pronounced. "You have courage."

"Well," I laughed, "you were the one who put me up to it. You have a strange power over me."

Maria laughed and looked away out the small plate-glass window into the lazy afternoon heat. A small oscillating fan in the restaurant tried to cool its patrons, but it was a charade. The air was saturated with humidity, and it was hard to do anything else but sit, which was fine by me.

Walking slowly back to my car, Maria seemed self-absorbed. I tried to engage her, but it was no use. We just strolled silently down the street, keeping a pace that avoided generating perspiration — a skill from the tropics I now embraced.

"Tell me, Nick," Maria said suddenly, "would you be interested in helping some of my student friends in the way you spoke about?"

"I'm not sure what you mean," I said, though my heart sunk with recognition. It was the part of my life that I did not want intertwined with Maria.

"Many days ago you showed me a photograph from the newspaper. The photograph we had taken from your car. At Miraflores. Do you remember?"

"Of course I do," I said.

"You said you would be happy to help my friends."

"Yes," I said.

"I have been asked to inquire if you would help them."

"Do you want me to help them?" I asked. A niggling thought wormed its way into my consciousness. Perhaps Maria's interest in me was less romantic and more professional after all.

"You may help them if you wish," she said. "It is not my decision. I have been asked to inquire."

"I'm honored to help any group you're involved with, Maria. You know that. What do you suggest I do?"

"It is not my decision," she repeated, waving her hand in agitation.

"Well, please tell your friends that I'm willing to help them."

She nodded and we walked back to the car in silence. I felt an odd sadness to the last exchange and realized Maria and I were veering in yet another, unexpected direction.

By the time we got back into the car, my back was coated with perspiration and it stuck awkwardly to the back of the car seat. Maria sat farther than normal across the cavernous front seat and offered up a fretful, distracted smile.

"Maria," I said at one point, deciding there was little to lose, "I see that your father is a powerful labor leader. Is that true?"

"Who told you that?" she shot back.

"Lots of people told me," I said. "Why are you surprised?"

"I do not want to talk about my father."

"OK," I said.

CHAPTER 30

The following Monday morning I was shaving in a fog smeared mirror when I heard knocking at the front door.

"Damn," I said, as I waddled to the peephole with shaving cream on my face and a towel around my waist.

Squinting through the peephole, I saw Maria. She had another young man with her who I did not recognize.

"Maria," I said opening the door. "I'm afraid you caught me a little off guard. I wasn't expecting you."

Standing in the doorway, she seemed very nervous and held both her hands together in front of her.

"We are so sorry to disturb you, Professor Baker," she said, reverting to an unexpected formality. "I would like to introduce to you Conrado Aguirre."

"Um, hello, Conrado," I said, feeling foolish in my state of attire. He shook my hand.

"May we come in?" he said firmly.

"Yes, please," I said, holding tightly onto my towel with my left hand. "But please give me a moment to clean up." I returned quickly to the bathroom, made a sweep of my stubble, avoiding the small scab that was the last vestige of my run in with the baseball-bat boys. I washed up and dressed in my bedroom. I could hear Maria and her friend speaking in hushed tones in the living room.

"So, what's up, Maria?" I said sitting on the couch.

"Do you remember when you said you would help our student group in a demonstration?"

"Yes, I do. I thought you said I could join you."

"Well, actually, the demonstration is today. But it is not a big demonstration. It is a little thing."

"But symbolic," Conrado said. "Very symbolic." He spoke English well. I tried to guess their relationship. I had never seen him before and Maria had never mentioned him. She appeared intense, nervous, and focused.

"Maria tells me that you had offered many times to help her and the cause of Panamanian independence," he said. Maria dropped her eyes.

"Maria is correct, of course. I have made the offer many times. How can I help you?"

"Maria said that you have a car. Is that correct?"

"Yes."

"Would you be willing to drive some students around the Canal Zone today? It would be better to have an American driving."

"I might be willing," I said carefully. "What are you planning to do over there?"

Conrado looked at Maria for reassurance and then back at me. "We are going to plant some Panamanian flags in the Canal Zone."

I almost laughed. "Excuse me? Plant flags? Why are you going to do that?"

"It is called 'Operation Sovereignty,'" Maria said.

"The Americans refuse to fly the Panamanian flag in the Canal Zone," he said leaning forward to the edge of the chair. "Even in Japan, the Americans fly the Japanese flag on their military bases. Japan is a defeated country and yet the Americans fly the Japanese flag. But here, they do not fly the flag of a friend – Panama. It is insulting. Today we will plant our flag there. Will you help us?"

"Absolutely," I said, "but on one condition."

"And what is that?" he said carefully.

"That you are not going to hurt any Americans or Panamanians, and that there will be no property damage of any consequence."

"You have my word," he said.

I looked at Maria, but she avoided eye contact again, so I stood up and said, "Let's get going then."

Operation Sovereignty was laughably tame, more like a Chinese fire drill. I drove two university students and Conrado through parts of the Canal Zone. They would jump out at intersections or public areas and quickly stab the small flagpoles into the grass, and we'd take off.

The Panamanian national flag is simple and elegant. It has four equal quadrants: the top left shows a blue star centered on a white background, with a counterbalancing red star on the bottom right. The bottom left quadrant is a solid blue box, while the top right shows a solid red box.

We planted flags in front of the Tivoli, at the base of the hill leading up to the administration building in Balboa, while two American kids on bikes laughed at us. Apparently, there were other teams simultaneously planting flags that day.

The few Americans in the Canal Zone who saw us seemed amused or uninterested. My one satisfaction from this event would be finally proving to Don that I had penetrated a leftist student group.

I dropped the Operation Sovereignty boys off at the university, and they thanked me profusely, leaving me with a Panamanian flag for solidarity. I stopped at a phone booth and employed the emergency protocol sequence. I called the pre-assigned number and asked the woman who answered if I could speak to the "operator." She said I had the wrong number and hung up. I called the same number a moment later and asked for the operator again. She repeated that I had the wrong number and hung up.

The gears were in motion. I slowly made my way to the Fort Amador Causeway, looping through Balboa Heights, down into Balboa, past the YMCA, and out past the yacht club to the overlook. I doubled-backed once for good measure before parking.

Don's car skidded in the loose gravel before halting. I sat on the hood of my car watching a US Navy destroyer exit the Canal to our right.

"What's going on?" Don said out of breath.

And I told him everything, the name of this new fellow, the students with the flags and where we had planted them. He wrote everything down on a small pad.

"So, is this flag thing 'it'?"

"For right now it is, though, they hardly shared everything with me. I consider it a good sign that they used me at all."

"So do I," Don said. "This is excellent. But you better get your ass out of here right now. No telling how they'll try to use you now."

If someone had told me that a bunch of small Panamanian flags — 72 to be exact — could lead to so much trouble I wouldn't have believed it.

The Canal Zone police, downplaying the incident, returned the flags to Panama. A spokesman for the Canal Zone administration said in the English language edition of the *Star & Herald*: "The action is ridiculous and not worthy of official notice."

The American embassy said they were monitoring the situation, and the State Department in Washington was quoted as saying it was nothing more than a "student prank."

I agreed, but of course, I was wrong.

The following day in class Maria came in late and sat near the front.

I handed back some graded papers and started my lecture when one of the students raised her hand. I acknowledged her.

"Professor Baker," she said, "is it true that you helped the students in Operation Sovereignty?"

"Gee, word travels fast," I said, glancing at Maria. She did not look happy.

"But yes, it's true," I said. "I was proud to take part in the demonstration. But it was a small part."

And then the students starting clapping, standing up, and whistling. I tried to quiet them but they only got louder. Finally, when they started to slow down, I went to the chalkboard and started to write down an assignment. Instead of quieting down, they started another round of raucous applause and whistles. I looked at Maria and she shrugged her shoulders.

I looked up at the small glass window on the door to the room and could see the professor from the next room peering in.

OK, I thought, that's it. I announced that the class was cancelled. There was more hooting and applause. Laughing, I collected my things and walked to the door. I looked at Maria, hoping she'd follow me out, but she didn't.

I went to my car, waited patiently for Maria, and finally left when she didn't show.

Later that afternoon a crowd estimated at around a thousand university students, marched on the Presidential Palace with the returned Panamanian flags as symbols of their earlier protest. They demanded that President de la Guardia speak to them, but he deferred, citing a sore throat. They wanted him to request that the Canal Zone fly the Panamanian flag. And for good measure, they demanded more funding for education and the ouster of the Education Minister.

Maria stopped by my apartment after the demonstration to tell me.

"I believe de la Guardia is scared of us now," she said. "He would not even talk to us. He was a coward."

"Whoa, Maria," I said. "You should be careful out there. I don't like the look of those National Guardsmen. I assumed you joined the march?"

"Yes."

"Well, do you think all this stuff is over now, or do you think it will continue?"

"Most certainly it will continue," she said, her eyes animated. "You will see."

As reluctant as I was to put on my spy hat, I did it nevertheless. "Maria, who is this Conrado? Is he a leader of the students?"

"Yes, of course."

"I see. Tell me, are there others involved in the organization? Non-students? People who are able to offer help to students. Perhaps with money?"

"Well, yes, I suppose there are some, like you, who help us."

"Besides me, who are they?"

"Lots of people. Too many."

"Are they all Panamanians?"

"Maybe others. Some from Colombia, I suppose. Costa Rica. Why do you ask?"

"Oh, I just wanted to see if I was alone," I said laughing. "The only westerner."

"Are you afraid to help us?" she said, standing up and walking towards me as I sat on the couch.

"No," I said, watching her carefully. If there's one thing I had learned about Maria, it's that she nearly always seemed to take charge. At this moment I was just an obedient schoolboy.

She gave me an impish look and unexpectedly dropped onto my lap, her legs falling down the length of the couch to my right. She put her arms around my neck and kissed my cheek, then rested her head on my shoulder and sighed.

I could feel her thighs pressing down on my lap. And while my body tingled with sexual excitement, I was vaguely unsettled by Maria's behavior. I had the unmistakable feeling of being manipulated, not that I minded. Still, it put me on guard, or as much as I could muster given the circumstances.

And then, to my amazement, she started crying. At first, I thought she was laughing, but she quickly buried her face in my neck and sobbed. I decided not to say anything. Her warm tears slid down my neck. Finally, I couldn't stand it any longer and craned my head to look at her.

"Maria, what are you doing?" I said. "What's wrong?"

Instead of answering me, she buried her face again on my shoulder and neck so that I couldn't see her face. I gave up and let her sit in my lap, sniffling next to my ear while I gently stroked her temple and forehead. I wiped a few tear streaks from her cheek.

I had no idea what was happening. We sat that way for about five minutes. Then she slowly raised herself to a sitting position. I looked into her watery, bloodshot eyes and she leaned down quickly and kissed me hard on the lips. Then she stood up, straightened her blouse and skirt absently, and then went over to grab her purse.

"Maria," I pleaded, "what's going on? Can't you tell me?"

"Nick," she said shaking her head sadly. "We can never be. Do you know that?"

"No," I said. "I do *not* know that. Who said we can't be in love? Where is that written?"

"For a grown man you are very naïve," she said. "You do not know very much about what is happening in Panama."

"So tell me, for god's sake, Maria!"

She looked at me again, sighed, and walked out of the apartment.

★

Maria said a larger demonstration was going to take place the following Monday. It was going to be a "peaceful" march near the Canal Zone. Students would gather in an open field several blocks south of the highway separating Panama City from the suburban Canal Zone neighborhood called Ancon.

She told me to wear loose-fitting clothes and tennis shoes if I had any.

Don was ecstatic when I reported the details in a dead-drop note. He insisted on meeting immediately.

"Goddamn, Haliday, see what happens when we put one of our own men on the ground?" he said at the Fort Amador causeway. "I've been trying to get stuff out of the locals, and they've given me squat. But you came right through!"

He pressed me on the source, and I admitted it was Maria.

"Stay close to her," he said. "She's important."

"I'm on it," I said.

Maria was standing in the street outside her house with Julio, the photographer when I pulled up Monday morning. They both rode in the back seat.

She looked nervous and barely spoke on the way in, while Julio acted like he was going to a major league baseball game.

He spoke quickly in Spanish, but she cut him off. "*En inglés*," she said.

"Maria," he started again, "how many of us will there be?"

"We don't know," she said.

"One thousand?"

"Julio, I don't know," she said.

"I'm going to take many pictures," he said proudly, staring out the window.

Several moments later, he started all over again.

"Will de la Guardia do anything?" he said. "They will not use their guns, yes?"

"No, why would they use guns at a peaceful march?" she said. "You worry too much. Take photographs. Everything will be fine."

I stole a glance in the rearview mirror at Maria. She stared straight ahead, her mouth taut at the edges. I preferred the softer side of Maria; the young revolutionary Maria was all business.

About ten blocks away from the gathering point, she directed me to park. We were situated in a dense, older area of Panama City. Two- and three-story stucco buildings with cast-iron railings hung over the streets. Residences were mixed in with retail shops and restaurants. The side streets were narrow, and we walked with other small groups to an open field.

The closer we got to the field, the more excitement I could feel. Nearly all the protesters were young men, most sporting the unofficial uniform of university students: white cotton shirts and long dark-blue pants. Maria was dressed similarly, with her hair pulled back in a pony-tail. She looked tomboyish and unbearably cute, except for that steely look on her face.

It was hard for me to get my bearings since I was not familiar with this part of the city. I couldn't tell whether we were two blocks or two miles from the border of the Canal Zone. The gathering point was a large dusty open field littered with bottles, rusting sheet metal, and the skeletal remains of automobiles.

We milled around the outskirts of the crowd, but soon got locked into the main group as more protesters filtered in behind us. A man yelled through a megaphone exhorting the crowd, but I couldn't un-derstand what he was saying. Maria kept tugging my shirt as she moved to make sure I kept up with her and Julio.

As the crowd pressed together tightly, I began to sweat heavily, feel-ing rivulets rolling down my back until they were absorbed into my cotton shirt. I took the opportunity, under cover of the pressing crowd, to reach out and hold on to Maria. I placed my hand on her hip, at the part that flared out from her waist. She didn't object, and as time wore on, I would sometimes hug her briefly against my hip, pressing our sweaty bodies together. Maria never pushed me away.

At one point we got separated in the crush, and she reached back and grabbed my hand like a parent worried about losing their child. She hung on tightly. We were pushed and pulled with the crowd of young people and held hands openly like young lovers.

After what seemed like an hour, the crowd — which I estimated at around 1,500 — did a sudden about face like a school of agitated anchovies. We found ourselves turning in the opposite direction and walking en masse up a large avenue. There was no way to tell where we were going or what our surroundings were because I could only see the people crushed in around us.

Finally, the crowd loosened up a bit and there was slightly more breathing space. I could now hear sirens coming from straight ahead. The crowd slowed and we found ourselves bumping into people who had stopped in front of us.

The feeling of claustrophobia and confusion began to get on my nerves. I could feel Maria's hand tighten around mine as she also sensed a change in the situation.

And as if Houdini himself had masterminded an extraordinary feat of magic, the buffer of young men in front of us evaporated until Maria and I, along with dozens of other startled protesters, found ourselves at the front of the pack staring into a perpendicular line of brown-shirted, helmeted Panamanian National Guardsmen. They were less than one hundred yards away. Beyond them, on the other side of the street, were white-helmeted policemen with blue shirts. They were American cops protecting the border.

The crowd pushed us onwards from behind, but we resisted. Then apparently, as the rows had done before us, Maria and I evaporated to the side and slid back along the outside of the crowd.

She and I had not exchanged a word in more than forty-five min-utes, communicating instead by pressing, pulling, and grasping each other in our alternating game of crowd management and flirtation.

We stood to the side, as the crowd surged forward, and I don't know which group looked more frightened, the young Panamanians pressing forward to the border or the young Panamanians with surplus M1 rifles trying to block them from reaching the border.

All attention was focused on the impending showdown in front of us. Not more than thirty feet behind us, a small cross street intersect-ed, and I really should have known better what was about to happen.

Maria was the first to go airborne — she flew awkwardly sideways, and I felt her hand ripped from mine. There was a confounding roar-ing sound and I felt a powerful force hit the center of my back that sent me flying face-first onto the street.

CHAPTER 31

A red Panama City firetruck was stationed at the cross street behind us and — camouflaged by the sounds of sirens and the crowd — had turned their hose on us.

Maria was back up on her feet in a flash and laughed briefly as she helped me up. By now the crowd was dispersing in wild surges as the demonstrators tried to avoid the hose, so we ran hand in hand to the other side of the street. Maria took yet another full burst of water on her back that knocked her down and under my feet. We tumbled, along with a shirtless young boy, into a soggy heap.

Staggering down a side street we stopped and laughed wildly at what seemed like child's play. Maria attended to a cut on my elbow and then marveled at how I was drenched on the entire back of my body — neck to feet — while I was bone dry on the front.

Maria, on the other hand, was completely drenched and I made a silly comment about seeing the label on her bra since her blouse was nearly transparent as it stuck to her skin.

"You are a dirty man," she said, slapping my wrist.

"Should we go back?" I said, looking down the small street to the commotion swirling on the main drag. "Let's leave. We've done our duty."

"We cannot stop now," she said. "My friends are there. I need to be with them."

"Well, do me a favor, Maria," I said holding her shoulders and forcing her to look at me. "If those goons from the National Guard start acting crazy, I'm dragging you away with my own two hands. ¿*Entiendes?*"

"You should not worry so much," she said, pulling me back down the street with her small but strong hands.

It was like walking onto a chaotic, high-speed highway; small gangs of young men were swirling past us, some moving up to the line of police, and others running away. The fire truck disappeared, thank god, and we briefly watched from the side street. Gangs of young men swept in front of the National Guard, and then peeled away like fighter jets on a bombing run.

To make matters more surreal, whole groups of non-protesting Panamanians, including businessmen, mothers with their children, and even some Americans, stood in small groups watching the wild action.

The soldiers were restrained, though every now and then one of them would briefly lower his rifle and make a gesture of aiming from his hip. But they never fired, nor did they budge.

Behind us, farther down the main street in the direction of our original advance, I could smell something pungent and turned to see a car burning brightly, heavy black smoking rising vertically into the humid air.

The frustration of the demonstrators began to vent itself on random objects. I heard a huge crash and saw a plate-glass store window collapse and for the first time saw a Panamanian police car, a two-toned Ford, race down the street and pull up in front of the storefront.

The crowd evaporated as the two policemen charged out of their vehicle. One of them brandished his revolver, wildly pointing it around.

"Maria, come on," I said, "Let's get out of here. I don't like this."

"No," she said firmly. "Come." At which point she tugged me down the street toward the burning vehicle — the precise direction I thought we should avoid. Nevertheless, feeling increasingly protective toward this woman — and oddly curious about her lack of fear — I allowed myself to be pulled toward trouble.

The earlier mob swarming behavior had changed from giddy excitement to something far different. Some of the agitators were throwing rocks, and there were many young boys now, running swiftly past the older protesters. The boys seemed more reckless, taunting the police more fiercely.

And just as quickly, the police left. The crowd now seemed intent on taunting the row of National Guardsmen near the border. A group spontaneously chose a parked car, rocking it furiously until it flipped over. Gas seeped out of its gas tank and some kid dropped a lighted match on the fuel.

I pulled Maria down another side street.

"Maria, I'm not allowing you to go back," I said, grabbing her wrist and hanging on tight.

"I am looking for someone," she said plaintively, trying to break my grip. "Why do you not let me look for him?"

"Julio? He'll be fine."

"No, not Julio. Someone else."

"Good lord, are you looking for your boyfriend?"

She gave me a look of disgust and then broke my hold on her wrist by twisting furiously. She took off running toward the action — again.

For a moment I considered not following her. But as soon as she turned the corner, I felt a flutter of panic and ran after her. By the time I rounded the corner she was gone, her white cotton shirt blending in with hundreds of white cotton shirts.

Staying to the side of the street, I jogged toward a roiling group of about fifty protesters who were now technically rioters. They were pushing an empty Oldsmobile toward a parked police car. Maria couldn't be too far ahead, so I just kept going, stumbling and bouncing off fleeing men and boys.

I saw a couple of men in front of me abruptly pull up short, as if they were puppets whose strings had been yanked back. Moments later I found myself bent over convulsively coughing and rubbing my eyes.

So now it was tear gas. Great, I thought. The "peaceful demonstration" was now a full-scale riot in Panama City. The protesters were angry at being blocked by the well-armed National Guard and were taking out their frustration on their city.

I pulled my shirt up over my mouth and started running past people on their knees convulsed in coughing fits. One shirtless boy was throwing up on the sidewalk. I kept rubbing my eyes hoping the stinging would stop, but it didn't.

And then I heard the unmistakable pop, pop, pop of M1s coming from up the road. Some idiot in the National Guard had given the order to fire. Where the hell was Maria? I took a left onto a side street and lingered there with what seemed like a tubercular ward of coughers. Many of the protesters were now done with this peaceful demonstration and were starting to filter in ones and twos away from the chaos, rubbing their eyes and hacking from the tear gas.

I yelled, "Maria! Maria!"

I got a few cursory glances from my fellow sufferers but that was it.

Walking away from the tear gas I took side streets to cut back and reenter the riot from up near the border. It took twenty minutes, but I finally emerged and mingled with a group of bystanders. Farther down the street there were swarms of men in pitched battles.

Across the street, on the American side, there was a large municipal building with the words Ancon Elementary School on it. Boy, I thought, I bet those kids had a surprise whiff of tear gas today.

I made another attempt to find Maria, and walked slowly down the hill, staying on the sidewalk and close to the buildings. There were now two burning cars and I heard jeering.

I kept scanning the crowds at the periphery, thinking that Maria would be there if she was anywhere. When I was about twenty yards away from the first burning vehicle, its gas tank exploded with a deep thud, sending dark black smoke curling straight up. There were more jeers, and someone threw a Molotov cocktail — the first one I had seen all day — right onto the hood of a police car that had just pulled up. It bounced innocently off to the side and lay there in the street burning morosely.

Four Panamanian policemen were in the car and they were enraged by the flaming missile thrown at their car. The driver jumped, out and I kicked myself for not running because he pulled out his revolver and emptied it wildly into the crowd. I saw one rioter wobble as if he'd been dosed with a tranquilizer, and then he fell face first onto the street.

One round must have hit the building about three feet above me, because I heard a thud and felt some plaster sprinkle on top of my head.

I ran with a huge crowd wildly down the side street and away from the burning cars. About two blocks later we all slowed down, trying to catch our breath. Several men around me were laughing nervously and looking back to see if they were being chased. Thank god we weren't. I had just about enough interaction with the Panamanian Police Department that day.

My right hand was suddenly grabbed from behind, and I twisted sideways in alarm, bowling into two men walking on my left.

It was Maria. Without uttering a word, she threw her arms around my chest, hugging me. It is odd how powerful small moments can be, but as I stood, being pressed up against the side of a tenement building by this small woman, I felt real joy. This was not a feeling I was used to and it left me tranquil and glassy eyed.

Maria finally let go and stood back to look at me.

"I was worried about you," she said. "I looked and could not find you. I asked Julio but he did not see you."

"Me?" I said laughing. "You were worried about me? Maria, I've been looking for you. Can we leave now?"

She nodded, turned, and starting running away from the burning cars. She tugged my right hand and I had no intention of letting it go. We jogged at least two blocks with her tugging me along until I finally stopped.

"Maria, it's OK. We can walk slower now. I think we're out of trouble."

She peered around my shoulder to make sure.

"Yes," she said. "We may walk."

The most amazing thing happened. She held onto my right hand and we sauntered openly, like lovers. Once we stopped at a traffic light as two police cars sped by, and she was not afraid to press up against my body, standing idly until we could cross.

Thank god, I kept telling myself, that Maria was a low-level agitator. I could pump her importance up with Don now to justify spending more time with her. But at some point, I'd explain to Don, that this woman Maria was simply not important enough to worry about.

We stopped in front of a drug store, and I said, "Let's get something to drink. Do you want a Coke?"

"Yes, please," she said. "I can still taste the gas."

We ambled inside. A vending machine sat against the wall and I put in a nickel and pulled a Coke out of the grip of two restraining bars; then I did it again. Off to the side in the store, I saw one of those photo kiosks that produce a bunch of black-and-white photos in a long strip.

"Maria," I said. "Come on."

When she saw where I was taking her, she dragged her feet. "Nick, no, no. I look very bad. Look at me."

"You look beautiful," I said. "Don't be silly. I want to remember you like this."

She fought me a bit more, then relented. I sat down on the small stool and pulled the curtain shut. An added bonus, I discovered brightly, was the fact that she would have to sit on my lap.

The first photo flashed while she was fussing with her hair and we laughed. The next one was very posed. For the next one, with my arms around her, I pulled her closer and she rested her head on my shoulder. It flashed again. She nuzzled closer and said, "You will keep these photographs secret, yes?"

"I'm going to send them in the mail to your mother, of course," I said.

Just as she twisted to look at me the flash went off.

"You are a bad man," she said, settling again. I rested my chin on the side of her head.

"For a woman who got tear-gassed today," I said, "you smell wonderful."

She sighed. The flash went off. She turned her face to look at me. In those awkward moments, before we kissed, I was incredibly happy.

We kissed hard, our teeth awkwardly clanging together. Then we kissed again, and this time it was soft. Our breathing was rapid. Sometimes one of us needed to break away just to catch a breath.

But it was wonderful and incredibly sexy. Then she did that little trick of grabbing my lower lip with her teeth and gently pulling. She was so accepting of my kisses that she kept repositioning herself in the tiny booth to allow us to kiss.

The curtain flap suddenly opened, and the manager stuck his head in, yelling in Spanish. Maria barked back at him as we untangled. Outside I quickly grabbed the curl of six photos and threw them in my top pocket. Maria fussed with her hair and straightened her cotton blouse. Two older women looked disapprovingly at us as we tumbled into the street, laughing like delinquents.

We walked hand in hand to my car, and she snuggled up to me as I drove, gently rubbing my arm with her hand.

I tried to talk her into coming back to my apartment, but she would just laugh, sigh, and say, "No."

"Oh, come on, Maria, we can watch TV," I said.

"You mean on the couch?" she said laughing

"Yes, why not?"

"I do not think so."

I gave up and just luxuriated in having her sit next to me, holding my hand. Like any man, I wanted more, of course. But it was just the beginning; I could see that.

When we were a couple of blocks from her home, she suddenly grew tense and slid away to the passenger side window.

"Too late," I said, "your mom just saw us holding hands."

She whipped her head around to look at the street, then back at me.

"You should stop that, Nick! You are causing me a lot of trouble."

"Well, I can't see your mother ever warming to me, that's for sure."

"I don't understand 'warming,'" she said.

"She doesn't like me now and never will," I said.

"We will change her mind," she said. "She will like you. I promise."

"Ha, I love that about you, Maria," I said with a tenderness that surprised me. "You are so determined."

"Do not talk in that way when we are so near to my house. It makes me want to kiss you again."

"Well, can I see you soon?" I said. "Tomorrow?"

"Yes, of course," she said getting out of the car. "Goodbye, Professor Baker. Thank you for the ride," she said loudly.

I watched her in the rearview mirror and nearly hit a car that had stopped in front of me. The driver, a man perhaps in his sixties, gesticulated wildly and commented on my poor driving by raising his middle finger.

CHAPTER 32

I was in my apartment no more than two minutes when the phone rang once and then stopped. A minute later it rang once and stopped. Then came a final third ring after another minute of silence.

Great, I thought, just great. It was the emergency communication that told me to get my butt to the overlook at the Fort Amador Causeway.

The drive was pleasant enough. The sun had set an hour earlier, and with the windows open, the evening was pleasant and cool. A stray shower had just lumbered past, and though the streets were wet, the air had not yet fouled from the brutal humidity.

I fantasized about Maria all the way there. I could literally feel her breath on my face. My car lights caught Don's darkened vehicle at the overlook. His cigarette glowed from inside the car, and I dutifully pulled up and joined him in the front seat of his Ford Fairlane.

I'm sure he couldn't wait to talk about the riot that he knew I had attended.

After the interior car light extinguished, Don said nothing. He just puffed away and stared at a small tanker traversing into the Pacific from our great American canal. The sparse navigational lights provided a surreal image as if the green and red lights were suspended magically above the water, floating in the air.

"Well," Don said almost to himself, "the consensus is that we could leave you there. You're not exposed. After this crap goes down, we think you can still stay at the university."

"Stay at the university? I'm not sure what you're talking about, Don, but I don't think my cover is blown. No need to change my assignment. Unless you know something I don't."

"Nope," said Don, blowing a huge stream of cigarette smoke out of the open window into the night air. A desultory breeze from the Pacific seemed to grab it reluctantly and wrestle it from the car.

Don was usually very angry, or just plain normal angry. But he was never silent.

"Well, those assholes sure got our attention, that's for sure," he finally said.

"Don, you talking about the demonstration today?"

"Of course I am!" he said, his voice rising. Now, this was the Don I could relate to. "Those stupid jerks really caused a stir. You know," he said turning in his seat to face me, "I just got off the fucking phone to Washington. There was a CBS news crew here and they put the demonstration on the evening news back home! In the United States! Can you believe it? What a goddamn mess. Man, are they pissed off."

"It'll calm down," I said. "I was there. It wasn't that bad. Just a couple of cars burned."

"Are you crazy, Haliday?" he said. "Do you know how many people were killed today?"

"I heard the firing but only saw one guy fall."

"There were eight people killed today; seven men and one woman. The woman was a bystander. Unbelievable. This is an unmitigated mess. And you know, Haliday, you didn't give me squat on what was happening. Where the hell was your intel on this thing today? Shit, my boss chewed me a new asshole. 'Don, what the fuck are you doing down there? Every member of Congress and even Eisenhower saw the news reports.'

"And do you know the worst part?" he asked, but of course he wasn't looking for an answer. "The worst part was the school kids."

"What school kids?"

"American school kids, Haliday. They tear-gassed American kids at an elementary school. The parents are absolutely wild. Those were our kids, American kids. Who the hell do they think they are?"

"Do you mean at that Ancon Elementary School? The one on the border?"

"Yep. Kids were throwing up and screaming for the mommies. It was awful."

"Any Americans killed today?" I asked. "You said eight were killed."

"No, all Panamanians."

We sat in the car looking out into the blackness of the Pacific. Don's cigarette ember reflected off the windshield like a miniature red sun.

"They'll be sorry tomorrow, that's for sure," he said. "Bunch of stupid wogs."

We stared into the Pacific Ocean some more.

"So," he said, "is there any reason we shouldn't send you back out? As far as we can see, you're clean as a whistle. Your cover's tight."

"I'm good. Unless you know something I don't?" I repeated.

"Well, it's just that it'll be kind of messy for a while. All those people disappearing. Bound to be some backlash. But like I said, we think you're fine."

"Don, I know I'm green at this stuff, but I'm confused. Who's disappearing? And what do you mean 'backlash'?"

"We've got Operation Banyan Tree underway. Some of the key people behind these riots are going to disappear. You need to know, but we can't see how you'd be associated with that. Just keep an eye out."

"What the hell is Operation Banyan Tree?"

"We're rolling up the opposition," he said. "Taking out the leadership. One fell swoop. Bang. In two days they'll all be gone."

"Gone? Who's going to be gone? The protesters? Don't be silly, there were thousands today."

Don laughed a short, truncated "Ha."

"You're a funny guy, Haliday. You worry me sometimes."

"Who's going to be gone tomorrow, Don?"

"The last count was twenty-seven. All leaders of the communist anti-canal movement."

"What the hell are you going doing with them?"

"I'm not doing anything. It's our partners. They'll take care of it."

"Who's our partners?"

"Colombians mostly. It's easier and cleaner for them to do this job. Within forty-eight hours these people will simply disappear off the face of the Earth. But man, will the ones left behind be shitting bricks!" Don made a vicious laugh.

"So Banyan Tree is this operation to 'disappear' twenty-seven Panamanians who have been leading this movement against the Canal Zone?"

"That is a roger," Don said. "Approved at the very top. No Suez Canal happening here."

And then, like a pot of water that takes forever to boil, the molecules in my brain heated up enough for me to steam out an important question. "Who's on the list? Anyone I know?"

"You most certainly do, now that I think of it," he said. "That girl's family. They're on the list. Sorry about that. Had to be done."

"Maria?" I said with too much emotion. "Maria and her family?"

"Relax," Don said reassuringly. "It'll be fine. The kids in your class won't blame you. Like I said, you're clean on this."

"But Don, are you saying that Maria and her parents are on the list to disappear?"

"Yeah, the girl, the mom, and the old man. The mom is not really involved, but we can't just leave her out there to complain. And of course, the old man is a piece of work."

"Are you sure you've got the right people? Maria's a nobody. So is her father. What the hell are you guys doing?"

"Hey, Lone Ranger, calm down. You think we're crazy? That family's in the middle of it."

"Don," I said grabbing his arm, "you're making a huge mistake. They have nothing to do with leading these students. For chrissakes, this is just crazy."

"Don't be a goddamn idiot, Haliday," he said, prying my fingers off his arm. "We've been watching the father for a while and we know he's no innocent bystander. And it helped that we flipped that other kid you told us about. The photographer."

"Julio?"

"Him, yes."

"You flipped him?"

"Yeah, and he was great. Dropped a dime on that girl. I mean we knew the dad was a bad one for sure, we just didn't know it was a family affair. Dad's getting funding from the Bulgarians here. I knew those assholes were up to something. Thank god you got that kid to us because we would have never picked out the girl. Good work on that."

I took several very deep breaths and tried to focus on the green light at the tail end of the tanker in the distance. It bobbed up and down slowly.

"You knew about Maria's father?"

"Yeah. One hundred percent certified communist agent, a well-funded labor leader. Bad guy."

"Why didn't you mention this earlier?"

"Compartmentalization. Didn't they teach you that? You need to know what you need to know, and nothing more. Can't have you giving away the operation if you were nabbed."

"And you're sure of the old man?"

"I can show you eight-by-ten glossies of him meeting one of the Bulgarians at a small restaurant in Colon. Very cute couple. The Bulgarian just happens to leave an envelope at the table when he leaves first. No, the old man's been watched for a while."

I looked out into the oily black Pacific Ocean, feeling a strange combination of anger and fear.

"They'll all disappear within forty-eight hours?"

"Yep. Starting in two nights. We're not losing this goddamn canal. You know," Don said, turning to me in the darkness of his car, "you did well on your first assignment. It may not look like much, but you did great. Now, remember, you go teach your classes like nothing's going on. These commies will reform around another group of leaders and hopefully, at some point, they'll turn to you again. Of course, the moment you feel some heat you pull your ripcord and get the hell out."

He patted me on the head like I was a puppy.

"What did you do to Julio?"

"The kid?"

"Yeah, him."

"Nothing. Just scared the shit out of him, gave him some money, and told him to keep feeding us information. And then he'll get more money. They like money, you know."

"You didn't hurt him, did you?"

"No, wasn't worth the effort."

"Gotta go," I said sliding out of the long front seat.

"Keep your head down," he said. "You're doing great."

CHAPTER 33

Sometimes the answer to a problem is hidden and you just need to hunt around, pick things up, and discard the useless items until you've found what you were looking for. I drove through the Canal Zone that night heading to Panama City in a panic, replaying over and over what I had just heard.

Maria would be dead in forty-eight hours! Jesus, how in the hell could that be? And it was me who had turned her and Julio over to the agency in the first place! How could I stop it and not be arrested or even killed in the process?

My stomach turned as I thought of Maria being jostled into a waiting car on her way to school, bound and gagged.

I pulled over to the side of the road and thought about an action plan, but the more I processed it, the more confused I got. And what if the Columbians were on their way to Maria's house right now? Maybe Don was lying to me. I looked at my watch — it was 8:45 p.m.

Who did I know that could help me? Who could dig me out of this jam? Seymour, my Camp Peary professor in spydom? He'd have me arrested. Don would have me shot.

Who then?

And there it was, like the title of a book that was staring at me from the shelf: my father. He was a big shot in the State Department. He knew everyone and was wise in these complicated international affairs.

I drove until I found a phone booth in the Canal Zone, got out, slid onto the stainless steel booth seat, and closed the glass louvered door. I pulled a weathered piece of paper from my wallet. It had my father's work number and the number at his Georgetown town house.

The operator put the call through, and I waited as the phone rang and rang. No one answered. The operator said, "It looks like no one's home. Please try your call later."

My father answered, groggy and hoarse.

"You have a collect call from a Mr. Nick Haliday. Will you accept the call?"

"Absolutely," he said clearing his throat.

"Father," I started blathering. It was amazing how quickly I could fall out of control. "I'm in trouble. I need your help. Oh god, what a mess I'm in."

"Jeeze, Nick, slow down. What's going on? Are you OK?"

And I told him everything, shamelessly telling him I was in love with this woman whose family was on a hit list assembled to "roll up" the Panamanian leftist opposition. The more I talked about what was happening the more hysterical I got.

"Nick," he finally yelled. "Nick, stop it. Just stop. Where are you?"

"In a phone booth. In the Canal Zone."

"Try to pay attention to me, OK? Just answer my questions very simply. OK?"

"Sure," I said, glad and willing to let him take control of my disassembling life.

"So you know for certain that the station chief there is organizing the disappearance of leftists in Panama? What did you say the name of the plan was?"

"He called it 'Operation Banyan Tree.'" I heard him rustling about for something.

"OK, got that. What is the name of this woman that you're concerned about?"

"Maria."

"No, Nick, her full name. Come on, concentrate."

"Oh, Santiago. Maria Santiago."

"Her father?"

"I don't know his first name."

"Their address?"

"Oh, um, let me think. It's 622 Arias Avenue. Yes, that's it. Panama City."

"Nick, give me the phone number at your phone booth."

I read it back to him and he repeated it to me.

"I'll call you back in ninety minutes," he said.

"Ninety minutes! They could be dead by then. What good is that?"

"Nick," he said firmly. "You need to collect yourself. There is nothing that I can do in less than ninety minutes. And even at that, I'm still not sure if I can do anything."

"Oh, great," I said. "Just great."

"Ninety minutes, Nick. Stand by that phone."

We rang off and I opened the booth door. Several large tropical insects were drawn to the light in the booth, and they raced for the bulb as if their entire existence depended on it. The light went out as I stepped outside, and they bounced around aimlessly.

I breathed the cool air and checked my watch. It was 8:50 p.m.

What can he possibly do to help? I thought. *Why am I sitting here for ninety minutes? She could be arrested and gone in that time!*

As time plodded on, I grew frustrated and anxious. In the wilds of my imagination, I envisioned Maria being killed by a bunch of Colombian assassins. It nearly drove me mad. I waited in the car for what seemed like forever, but only thirty minutes had passed.

I then hatched an outrageously stupid scheme to go back to my apartment and retrieve my gun, whereupon I'd stake out Maria's home and wait for her kidnappers to show. Then I'd save her and her parents.

Just me. No backup. In the process, I might end up killing contractors of the Central Intelligence Agency. Good move. Maria and I would live happily ever after in a Central American prison.

The phone booth's ring startled me, and I bolted to the booth, swung open the accordion glass doors, and grabbed the handset.

"Hello?" I bleated.

"Nick, are you alone?"

"Yes, of course, I am."

"OK, I've put together something for you. Have you calmed down?"

"Yes," I lied.

"All right. Before I start, I have to ask you a question. It's a simple question, but I want you to answer it soberly and honestly. By the way, have you been drinking?"

"No!"

"Good. Then here's the question. This woman — Maria — are you in love with her?"

"Yes."

"No, Nick. I mean *really* in love with her. Could you see spending the rest of your life with her, for instance?"

"What kind of stupid question is that?" I howled. "Father, what the heck are talking about?"

"Nick, this is a serious situation you've got yourself into. And in case you hadn't thought of it — and I doubt if you did — my position in the State Department is profoundly compromised by your predicament. To put it bluntly, Nick, it's illegal for me to counsel you to evade your responsibility as an agent for one of our clandestine government agencies. My career could be ruined if any of this was traced to me. Do you get my drift, Nick? I would do anything to help you, and you know that. But you've put me at a huge disadvantage here."

"Father, don't worry about your *career*," I said with petulant sarcasm.

He sighed deeply and then started. "OK, Nick, have it your way.

Fine. Here we go. This is all I have for you. The only way for you to save this girl Maria and her family on this short of notice is for you to come clean to them. Immediately. If you use some other method of communicating — like a note or some such thing — they'll ruminate forever and not act fast enough. They don't have forever. I've verified the operation, Nick. It is indeed called Banyan Tree. This woman Maria and her family are targeted."

"How did you find that out?" I asked.

"Oh heavens, Nick. Just pay attention to me. Here's the plan: You drive over there right now. Wake up the family if you have to. Their house is probably being watched, so you need to figure out how to get to them without being seen. This plan is null and void, not to say treasonous if you're seen tipping them off. You understand?"

"Yes."

"Once you're there, take Maria and her father outside into their backyard, and tell them straight up that you're an agent for the US government. Tell them they need to leave immediately or else they're dead. Tell them a squad of assassins has already been dispatched."

"Why the backyard?" I said.

"They're probably bugged inside, that's why. This woman's father has been under surveillance for a while. He's a paid operative of an East European security service. It's true. They've been watching him for years. I feel very, very funny helping him escape."

"What about Maria? Did you find anything out about her? Is she really involved?"

"Yes, she is. Sorry. But remember, get them to the backyard."

"What if they don't believe me?"

"Make them believe you, Nick. It's your only chance. And now, here's the really important part, son. You listening?"

"Yes."

"You walk out of there, get in your car, and drive directly to the Canal Zone. Find someplace to stay. Or tell your boss that your cover's blown. Anything. Just stay out of Panama from the moment you tell this woman and her father. Don't dare go to your apartment. And one more thing — and this you must promise me — after leaving them, you will not try to contact Maria, or rendezvous later. Nothing like that. To save her, you're going to have to let her go forever. But once her father knows who you are, you're fair game for all the foreign security forces down there working against us. Do you understand what I'm talking about?"

"Yes, I understand."

"Promise me you won't try to contact her."

"Don't worry. I'm not that stupid."

"Call me tonight when you get back to the Canal Zone please, Nick. I need to know you're safe."

"OK, Father. Thanks for your help. I mean it. You're incredible."

CHAPTER 34

There were lights on inside Maria's house when I drove by. It was past 11 p.m. and I scanned the parked cars in the street. Sure enough, there were two men sitting in a car a half-block back, smoking cigarettes.

I drove around the block and down the next street that ran parallel to Maria's. I counted the number of houses, and when I came to number five, I parked. If the house lots were all pretty much the same size, this house should abut Maria's backyard. And if they weren't the same size lots, well, then things would be more complicated.

Praying for a complete absence of canines, I raced down the driveway, past two parked cars, and over a small gate. So far, no dog. Moving to my left, I followed the stucco wall that seemed to demarcate many Panamanian house lots. At the far corner, after going through and around bushes and small trees, I jumped up to get my stomach on top of the wall.

I looked at the backyard of the house to my left and right. I couldn't tell if either house was Maria's. I chose the house on the left. Rolling my body over I fell onto a large bush and sat there for a moment to get my bearings. A dog started barking several doors down to my right, and I froze, hidden, I hoped, by the bush.

The dog put up quite a show and the light came on at the back of the house that I had invaded. A woman peered intently out into the yard, scanning. It was Maria's mother. After a minute the dog stopped barking and Mrs. Santiago closed the door.

While hiding in the bush, I had mixed feelings about helping Maria's father. Mr. Santiago, a paid agitator for a Communist spy ring? Sitting curled up behind the bush I couldn't help thinking I had missed something. If Maria's father was a paid agent, and a leader of a cell at that, then what did that make Maria? Had my original suspicions been correct — that Maria had been ordered to flirt with the young American professor so that he could be flipped?

And why was Maria so interested in attending the demonstration? Did her father expect her to report back to him?

Was something as innocuous as puppy love derailing the master plans of two huge, powerful, and dangerous organizations? A poorly motivated CIA field agent had met his match in a beautiful, purposeful operative for the liberation of Panama and the nationalization of the Panama Canal.

Or was that even true? Was Maria using me, or was she in love with me? She kept warning me about something, which I took to mean her family's hard-core resistance to me. Maria: operative, lover, or both?

My naïve and starved heart told me she was in love with me. The way she hugged and kissed me that day *had to be authentic*. What could be more real than that? In my short, discontented life, there were few things I believed in right then besides Maria's love.

I needed to get moving since those guys in the car in front of their house probably were part of the hit squad.

I moved quickly to the back door. Putting my ear against it I heard voices. Please, I prayed, let this *not* be a huge mistake.

I knocked.

Nothing happened. After a minute I tried again.

Still nothing.

I pounded this time and heard voices and footsteps. A man I did not recognize pulled the small curtain from the glass at the top of the door and stared at me. Then he turned and yelled something. Mr. Santiago puttered down the hallway, looked at me quizzically, then opened the door.

"Professor Baker, yes?" he said squinting into the glare of the outside light.

"Yes, it's Nick Baker, Mr. Santiago."

"Please tell me what you are doing in my backyard. Did you get lost? I do not understand."

"Mr. Santiago, I need to speak to you in private. It's very important. And I need Maria to join us. Right now. It's important. Please?"

"Professor Baker, if you do not mind, would you please come back tomorrow? This is not a good situation tonight. We are very busy. Please come back tomorrow." At that, he tried to close the door, but I had stuck my foot in the opening, and he peered down at it. I remained outside in the yard, and he appeared very angry.

"Professor Baker," he said, barely controlling himself. "You must leave." He said something to the man behind him and opened the door to let the man out. About my size, he grabbed my left wrist with his left hand and slipped his right hand behind my neck to grab my shirt collar. He shoved me away from the back door and into the yard.

It would be fair and even accurate to say that at Camp Peary I had learned precious little about the fine art of hand-to-hand combat.

So I was amazed — thrilled really — when I swung at him and hit the guy on his Adam's apple. He stopped dead in his tracks as if he'd been hit with a poison dart. I meant to hit his chin, but serendipity appeared to be on my side. He gave me the oddest look, then sank hard to his knees, grabbing his throat and making a gurgling sound. I kneed him on the right side of his temple, and he went flat out.

I had never used my knees for a weapon in my entire life, except at that moment. I can't even explain why I *thought* I could use my right knee against his left temple. But there you have it: strange things occurring on a strange night in the tropics.

I turned to look at Mr. Santiago.

"You are in grave danger, Mr. Santiago," I said steadily. "There is no time to waste. Are you going to let me save your family or are you going to call more of your soldiers? I will do the same thing to them if I have to." Don't even ask where *that* machismo came from. It felt good saying it because I was scared to death.

"Who are you, Professor Baker?" he said. "Why are you assaulting my house?"

"I need to talk to you and Maria. It has to be both of you. Right here. Right now. I'm going to save your life and you're going to let me. Do you understand?"

He just stared at me, apparently trying to figure out what to do.

"Now, Mr. Santiago! We're running out of time."

His wounded soldier groaned but just lay there. Santiago looked at him, then at me.

"Why do you need to tell Maria? You can tell me," he said.

"I'm in love with Maria. I need her to hear this."

He gave me a funny look, turned down the hallway and was met by two men I did not recognize. One of them had a handgun and my knees buckled. But Santiago barked at them and they stood off.

"Maria!" he shouted. "Maria. *Ven aquí!*"

We all waited — Santiago, his two goons inside the door eyeing me nervously, me, and maybe even the guy on the ground — for Maria to show herself.

She came down the crowded hallway and looked confused. She said something I couldn't understand, and squinting into the darkness, she stepped outside.

"Nick," she said. "What are you doing here in the back of the house?" She looked at her father for guidance, but he simply glared at me.

"Maria, I'd like to talk to you and your father. Alone. It's very important."

"We are here, Professor Baker," Mr. Santiago said impatiently. "Please tell us what you need to say."

"We need privacy," I said. "Let's stand over here." At that, I walked a few steps into the yard, and Mr. Santiago sighed loudly in frustration as he followed. I reached out and grabbed Maria's hand to tug her along.

I had palmed a small folded piece of paper in my hand and pressed it into her hand. She looked at me sideways but mercifully didn't acknowledge the paper. I dropped her hand and stood in front of them. The two soldiers stood inside the screen door, visibly agitated by all the strange activity and the vulnerability of their charge.

"Mr. Santiago, Maria," I said looking at them in turn, "I am not a professor. I am an agent for the United States Central Intelligence Agency. I am a spy. My mission was to penetrate the leftist groups at the university."

Even in the harsh binary lighting of the backyard — complete darkness on one side and the glare from the outdoor light on the other side — Mr. Santiago's face hardened perceptibly. He made a small involuntary twitch toward the back door where his guards stood.

Maria stepped closer to her father. Her mouth opened slightly, and her eyes widened.

"The demonstration today was not received well by the American government in Washington," I said quickly. "They are worried about the canal. There is a plan to remove many key members of the anti-American movement in Panama. The mission is already underway. You are on the list, Mr. Santiago. So are you, Maria."

"Professor Baker" — he caught himself and said derisively — "Mr. Gringo Spy, what do you mean 'remove'? We are not familiar with your quaint ways of speaking."

"Kill," I said, a little too harshly. "You, your wife, and Maria are on a list for assassination." Maria took yet another step closer to her father. The two guards had noticed Maria's alarm, so they opened the door and started toward us.

Mr. Santiago, to my relief, barked at them, and they went back inside.

"Why are you telling us this information?" he said, his jaw tightening. "You do not seem like a spy to me. You are a typical Yanqui who sees Latins as too emotional and stupid. And you are taken in by our women." He glanced at Maria and she lowered her eyes.

"Mr. Santiago, you have no time to argue with me. You must leave immediately. Please just disappear. If you don't believe me, what harm could hiding out for a few days do? Get out of here. Now. There are two men down the street watching your house right now."

Again, he made an involuntary twitch in the direction of his house, then refocused on me.

"So please explain again — why are you telling us this information, if you are indeed a spy?"

"I told you. I'm in love with Maria. I'll admit it sounds strange, but you have to believe me, it was not my intention to fall in love with your daughter. It has complicated my mission tremendously. Not only are you two in danger, but now I am equally exposed."

I looked at Maria and her eyes were wet with emotion. She raised her hands to her mouth.

"You are a spy?" she blurted. "You were spying on me? My family? My friends? For the United States?"

"Yes," I said. "But let's not be too high and mighty about this, Maria. I think your father encouraged you to stay close to me in case I proved useful. And he's been receiving support and funds from Eastern Bloc countries for some time."

Mr. Santiago made what sounded like a low hum and squinted sharply at me in the dark. He turned to leave, grabbing Maria's arm, but stopped.

"You know, love is a very mysterious thing, yes? We thank you for trying to help us. But please be forewarned, I cannot guarantee the same courtesy. I recommend you leave immediately because some people I know will be looking for you in just a few minutes."

"*Papá!*" Maria said, grabbing his hand.

"Maria, he is our enemy — " but that was all I heard because I had started running to the back of the yard and jumped over the wall landing ingloriously on top of a hibiscus bush. The blossoms had closed for the night, but I later found that my cheek had been forcefully pollinated with a smear of yellow dust.

CHAPTER 35

The restaurant was a small local place at the edge of Old Panama. Like a good operative, I made sure the kitchen had a rear entrance that would offer emergency egress.

I parked myself at the back with a good view of the entrance and within range of the small, cluttered kitchen. There were a few people eating.

I ordered a beer and some fried plantains, and waited.

There was no telling whether Maria was going to follow the directions in my note to meet here at 8 p.m. the following evening. I had hung out in the Canal Zone all day, keeping away from Don until I slipped across the border in the evening. It was crazy to think she'd be able to break away unseen, and even crazier to imagine after my confession that she wouldn't just turn the note over to her father.

Ah, but as her father had said, love is a mysterious thing.

The fact that I was breaking my promise to my father did not really resonate, nor that I was breaking my oath to the agency. I didn't care much about anything except seeing Maria again. At this point in my young life, her affection had the gravitational power of a hundred suns.

At 8:15 I became nervous. Only one group had entered the restaurant since I arrived. A family of four was busy chatting and working their way through a meal. Two young men had just paid and left. A couple in their fifties sat nearest me, saying almost nothing to each other.

At 8:20 I made the decision to leave, but I was not going out the front door. A pervasive sense of alarm had settled over me, and I was now aware of my dangerously reckless behavior. Sweat built on my stupid, love-crazed forehead.

I threw down a couple of dollars, and just as I turned to head to the kitchen, Maria walked in.

The look on her face was an odd mixture of anger and relief, almost like a parent who has just discovered a missing child. She walked over and sat down. Neither of us spoke.

Finally, in a tone of voice softer than I expected, she said, "You are a crazy man, Nick. Very crazy."

"I told you I'm in love. What can I say?"

She shook her head slowly and sighed. "My world is not good today. I am scared and tired. Many things are happening."

"Thanks for coming," I said, trying to get her to look at me. "I was hoping to see you one last time. I know this is a selfish question. And under the circumstances, probably a crazy question. But I needed to know."

"What? What are you asking? What do you need to know?" she said.

"Do you love me?"

She sighed, her shoulders dropped, and she reached her hand across the table and placed it on top of mine. "Of course, Nick. Why would I be here? My father is going to kill me, but I did it anyway."

"Maria, you know it wasn't supposed to be this way. To be honest, this is my first assignment for my government — and undoubtedly my last — but I just wasn't prepared for you, of all people."

"Me? You talk funny sometimes."

"You are so unusual and special, Maria. And beautiful."

Her eyes welled up and she sighed again.

"Why do you say such things about me?" she said, almost plain-tively. "You don't know me. I am just a girl. You confuse me so much."

"Maria, I needed to see you one more time to tell you I loved you and to ask if you loved me. It's that simple. Maybe one day in the future we will find each other. Away from this stuff. Do you think that's possible?"

"Oh, Nick, you are such a romantic," she said smiling sadly. "I guess it is possible. But please don't think of that now. You must get out of Panama. Now. My father is very angry, and he has told many people about you. They are looking for you. So please go now. Yes?"

I saw two men enter and sit at a table near the door.

One of Seymour's dictums was: "An operative can always spot an-other operative. You'll know one when you see one. They're profession-al fakers just like you."

These two guys were killers. The one facing me had a thin pencil mustache, neatly parted short brown hair, and even across the room, I could see his dark, reptile eyes.

I was unarmed because I had abandoned my apartment as my fa-ther suggested, but had not abandoned Maria, as he had also suggested.

The two men presented a quandary — who was the prey? Maria or me? This could be the CIA's hit squad — the blue team, my team — that had followed her. Or it could be her father's comrades — the red team — who had stumbled upon their prize catch, which was me.

"Maria," I said maintaining eye contact, "please pay careful atten-tion. I'm sorry but our luck has run out. There are two men who just sat down by the door — no, don't look — and to be honest, unless you can identify them, there is no way to tell who they're after. The bath-room's in the back. In a moment, could you please visit the bathroom? On the way back try to steal a glance at the men but avoid eye contact with the one facing me. He'll know right away that we're on to him. Try to be natural."

She looked at me and smiled wanly. "I am not frightened, Nick."

"Good," I said holding her hand, "because I am. Remember, act natural."

She stood up, and as she walked past me, she let her hand trail on my shoulder and her fingers grabbed my earlobe in a playful tug.

Well, that was natural, I guess.

I polished off the beer and raised the empty bottle to the waiter, and he nodded. Just as he put the fresh beer down, another man entered the restaurant, and he sat between our table and the two goons near the entrance.

The only problem was that he had the same look as the other two. We had a conflagration of liars, thieves, and killers in the same little, warm, humid Panamanian restaurant. There might have been a disturbance somewhere in the cosmos given the critical mass of evil in that little room.

Even the waiter seemed unnerved, and his eyes kept jumping as he took the order from the newcomer.

I studied the beer bottle in my hands, turning it slowly and feeling the cold condensation on the bottle tempering the hot perspiration from my palms. How the hell were Maria and I going to get out of this room without being killed?

She sat back down after her bathroom venture and grabbed my hand. "I do not know them," she said quietly.

"How about the fellow at that table," I said rubbing her hands and nodding.

"No."

Using the Camp Peary lessons, I needed just three things: (1) a diversion; (2) a head start; and (3) an obstruction for my followers.

"Maria," I said, holding her right hand cupped in my two hands, "I'm sorry for pulling you here this evening. I'm so selfish sometimes I can hardly believe it. Now I need to save you if it's the last thing I do."

"You are talking crazy again," she said. "Stop talking the crazy talk,

Nick. I will not let you protect me. What is the point of that? Perhaps I will run away, but you will stay? And you will die to save me? *No, seria estúpido.*"

"Do we have to argue about this?" I said.

"I will not let you stay."

"So, are we just going to stay here until the restaurant closes? They'll just grab us at the front door."

"I don't know. But I am not letting you stay to save me."

"Can I ask a personal question," I said leaning closer to her.

"Yes," she said moving her head to mine.

"Do you have a gun?" I said, trying to smile.

"Ha," she said. "You are a funny man, Nick. No, I do not have a gun."

We stared at each other, our faces only inches away.

"I do love you, Nick. But I am scared for you now. Why did it have to happen this way?"

Leaning forward the last couple of inches I turned my head slightly and kissed her gently. Then we kissed again. We sat back and stared into each other's eyes like sick little lovebirds.

Maria's eyes were now welling up and she quickly wiped the corner of her eye.

"Maria, I think we should make a run for it. It's our only chance. We need to keep leaning in like this as I explain my silly plan. They'll think we're talking love talk."

"But we are talking love talk," she said.

"Yes, that's true."

And then I explained my plan to her, and she just nodded, holding and patting my hand gently.

"Were you listening?" I asked. "Did you get all that?"

"Yes. Why? Do you not believe I am listening?"

"Well, you seem distracted."

And she repeated the plan, word for word.

"I'm impressed," I said. "You know, we should really get this thing started. My knees are shaking."

"Not yet," she said.

"Yes, Maria. We're running out of time. Even the owner of this joint knows something's up. We need to act."

"Tell me one more time."

"OK; I love you. I would love to marry you right now. I'd like to have children with you. Little Marias."

"And little Nicks."

"I don't think the world needs any more little Nicks. One of them is enough. All they do is screw things up badly." And I meant it.

"Are you ready?" I asked impatiently.

Maria sighed and nodded, but not before wiping the corner of her eye. "I am trying to be brave, Nick."

CHAPTER 36

Maria started sobbing loudly. Then she stood, wiping her eyes, and walked back to the bathroom.

All eyes were on Maria: the older couple behind us, the family of four, the killers at the door, the solo killer between us. Even the cook stuck his sweaty head out of the kitchen. Maria slammed the bathroom door, but you could hear her crying still.

So far, so good.

I downed the beer because I needed an empty bottle.

The waiter came over to the table and I pointed to the beers and plantains.

"*Tres dólares, treinta y cinco centavos,*" he said.

Out of the corner my eye, I saw Maria open the bathroom door and slide over to the kitchen.

"Hey, where's my money?" I yelled, reaching into my pockets. "Hey, who stole my money!"

The waiter could not speak English, apparently, though he got the drift of my complaint. He stood to my left, almost directly in front of the table with the solo spook. This guy was closest to me and was my biggest problem; the two goons at the door were secondary at this point.

I stood up with the beer bottle in my right hand, and the waiter stepped back. I could not have positioned him better.

Stepping forward with my full weight, I shoved the waiter backward onto the solo spook. And winding up like a baseball pitcher on a pick-off play, I threw the beer bottle at the head of the mustached goon at the door.

By the time the bottle shattered against the wall near his head Maria and I were pushing the startled cook out the back door into the alley.

Racing up the black alleyway, I could see the lights of cars whizzing by on the main cross-street ahead. We were halfway to the end of the street when I heard a huge commotion behind us as our pursuers poured out of the kitchen.

I heard several dull popping sounds, the telltale muffled retort of a silenced handgun.

It was just a hard tap, like an irate Catholic teacher's swipe on the shoulder of a sinning student. And it didn't hurt. But something hit me.

I slowed momentarily and then started running full bore again toward the street. Maria was incredibly fast and was on my right. We were only ten paces or so from the end of the alley. I grabbed her swinging hand to tug her hard left and away from all this craziness.

I believe I was actually smiling when we made it to the street, not believing that I pulled off this outrageous feat. And I had Maria in my hand, to boot!

Which explains why I couldn't protect myself when the guy who'd been hiding behind the corner stepped out and hit me so hard at the belt level that I was briefly airborne.

The force of his swing, coupled with my forward motion, created an awful lot of energy and I nearly fainted in pain. I found myself on my knees holding my stomach. Everyone in Panama, it seemed, started a fight by crushing your stomach. He hit me very hard on the jaw, generating — I kid you not — bright yellow stars in my fading vision. And as I fell over on my side, I saw another man holding a greatly distressed Maria who was screaming.

I'm embarrassed to say I did nothing to help Maria. Someone knelt hard on my back, crushing me into the damp cement sidewalk. He turned me over, punched me in the face to encourage compliance, I guess, and handcuffed me like he was roping and tying a calf. A dumb, stupid, reckless, hopelessly in love, pretend bull.

I felt my body being lifted, like a sack of cement, and carried over to an open trunk. As I was dropped in headfirst, I caught a glimpse towards the sidewalk of a man shoving Maria out of the way.

The trunk closed loudly, doors slammed, and the car drove off. The only other sound, besides the high-pitched hum of the tires on the road, was the muffled laughter of the men in the car. Laughter, presumably, at how easy it was to catch an American spy.

The only consolation I could muster, rolling around in the back of the huge trunk of the car, was that they wanted nothing to do with Maria. They just tossed her aside at the end after they got their prize. It was a Red team operation after all.

My left shoulder was wet and starting to sting. So what if I had been shot? I was a dead guy anyway. Besides, I deserved it. Seymour had warned that the best outcome would be if the captured agent is summarily executed: a shot to the head, a final back-up to the heart. That way the poor agent would be spared a messy interrogation.

"Don't think you won't talk," Seymour said. "Don't even think about holding out. They use drugs, or just unbelievable pain — like taking a hammer and smashing each finger. One at a time. Do you know how many nerve endings you have in your fingertips? By the time you wake up, you'll gladly cut off your own hand with a hacksaw."

I consoled myself in the darkness of the trunk by thinking of Maria. At least she was safe.

And oddly, the more I thought of Maria, the more I wanted to live. I noticed, interestingly, that the car was still in the city. There were many stop lights, and I could hear cars and buses all around me.

I quietly stretched and twisted to investigate the trunk. I performed the only trick I could remember with handcuffs: I used saliva to lubricate one of my wrists, slobbering it on, even licking it at one point.

Like a young child at Christmas who opens a wrapped gift and finds *exactly what he wanted*, the cuff on my left wrist slid off after only about five minutes of work. Not without taking some skin with it, but still, it was off.

I noticed something else. Whenever the car's brake lights were engaged, it created a mild glow inside the trunk, and I could see briefly. I started looking around in the trunk for anything I could use as a tool.

There was a tire spanner and a jack, but that was all. And then poking my fingers down the side cavity, I found a large screwdriver. I positioned myself at the trunk lock, and each time the brake lights illuminated, I tried to figure out how to depress the spring-loaded trunk lock.

Miraculously, the car still seemed to be in the city. Where the hell were they taking me? To the Bulgarian Embassy?

The car stopped at a traffic light. I decided to press hard onto the lock spring with the screwdriver. The trunk popped open, like the yawning mouth of a hippopotamus. I rolled out and stumbled onto the hood of the car behind. The driver looked like he was going to faint.

I heard car doors open behind me as I took off into the traffic. Blinded by the headlights, I dodged several cars and ran until I thought I was going to pass out. Then, to test my theory that I had escaped them, I ducked into a small pharmacy and stood back from the plate-glass window watching the pedestrians. I must have waited for ten minutes, huffing to regain my breath and fingering a swollen lip.

There were no bad guys following me. Unbelievable as it seemed, I was clear.

I turned around and standing behind the counter were the pharmacist and his female assistant. Their mouths were open in pure fear.

I had one handcuff attached to my right hand, and my left shoulder and back were soaked in bright fresh blood.

"*Hola,*" I said.

The pharmacist nodded a faint, nervous acknowledgment.

I left and walked until I could find a pay phone and made the emergency call sequence. I was connected to a young woman. I identified myself and said I needed to be picked up. I added that I was injured. She asked me, rather dispassionately, to describe the injury and whether it was life threatening.

I said it wasn't. I gave her an intersection and a description of what I was wearing.

And that was it. In thirty-eight minutes according to my watch, I was picked up by boatloads of men in three black Chevrolets. I was driven to Gorgas Hospital in the Canal Zone, sitting up on a hill overlooking twinkling, effervescent Panama City.

The ER physician told me they needed to remove a bullet fragment from the shoulder blade. Before the nurse applied the sickening drops of ether to the gauze mask, I felt Don's hand on my shoulder.

"You're gonna be fine, soldier," he said proudly.

The nurse asked me to count to ten. At number nine I was mercifully delivered from this odd day. A palpable and unpleasant blackness surrounded me. I could see huge yellow letters, like Broadway lights, spelling "HELP."

CHAPTER 37

Can you predict the trajectory of a life, based on early poor judgment and happenstance? Do bad things happen to people who deserve it? I don't think so, primarily because of what happened next.

They made me a hero.

Well, not in the newspapers or anything public like that, but within the agency. Don pushed for it, and some folks back in Washington thought it was a good idea to show how fortitude, courage under fire, and inventiveness could be applied in the direst circumstances to produce a positive result. Plus, I gather they were looking for heroes to pump up the troops.

Don never asked how my cover got blown. I said that it must have been one of the students, and he just shrugged.

"Bastards," he said.

The after-action interview that was held in my secure room at Gorgas Hospital was very cursory. The young man who conducted it tried to drill into niggling inconsistencies with my story, but Don wouldn't let him pursue those lines of questioning.

"Jesus Christ, you're going to throw him into a coma," Don yelled at one point. "Why don't you just pull out his IV? Would that make it easier for you?"

The young functionary departed soon afterwards, and Don told me not to worry. "Operation Banyan Tree was a smashing success," he assured me. "Those remaining Red agitators are hiding out in the jungle, man. I think they know we're playing for keeps with the canal."

Staring at the ceiling fan above, the blades swinging lazily round and round, I said nonchalantly, "So we got all our targets?"

"Hell no," he said. "You never get them all. But we got the big ones, that's for sure. Poof. They just disappeared and every commie out there is quaking."

"That's great. Well done."

"Something went wrong somewhere, Haliday, but with so many moving parts it's hard to keep a lid on plans like this. Someone dropped a dime on you but thank god we got you out."

"Who was it?" I asked. "Do you have any idea?"

"Washington thinks it was someone from one of the hit teams, but I don't know. I think it was closer, one of the locals. Could have been the runner who ran into you at the dead drop. Remember him?"

"Yeah."

"He's under a banana tree right now, providing solid nutrition," he laughed.

"You took him out?" I asked.

"Yep. No need to have someone like that around. You break the rules, you pay."

"Right," I said.

"Still, it would have been better to get them all," he said, standing up to leave. "Including that labor leader and his family."

"They got away?" I said.

"That guy had good sources, I can tell you that. They cleared out so fast they left water boiling on the stove and all the lights on. But it's OK. We'll get them. You don't screw with Uncle Sam."

"Right."

★

John Foster Dulles gave me a medal at an all-agency ceremony in Washington. The CIA hadn't moved to Langley yet — that was later in 1961 — but the auditorium near Constitution Avenue was packed.

My father was there, which was nice. I was happy to see him. With barely a year under my belt in the agency, I really didn't know anyone else except a couple of guys from Camp Peary.

Seymour, my trusty teacher, was there, and we had a good laugh about my accelerated training program. Of course, you can always laugh when the outcome is good.

Our fearless leader Dulles gave a terrific speech about the dangers of the worldwide communist conspiracy. He grandly segued into the awards he was presenting that day. I was one of six employees to be held out as examples of the best the agency had to offer.

I was the last recipient, right after the European specialist who, working around the clock, had single-handedly rooted out a mole in the US Embassy in Bonn.

"And finally," Dulles said, smiling broadly and turning to me, "there is Nicholas Haliday. You know, we rushed young Haliday into action in Panama, ladies and gentlemen, putting him undercover in an extremely exposed position. He provided critical intelligence for an important operation, but after having his cover blown by a double agent, he was kidnapped. And on his way to brutal interrogation and certain death, Haliday, using all the skills imparted to him at Camp Peary, was able to extract himself successfully from his kidnappers. And he did all this after suffering a gunshot wound. Now, I think you'll agree with me that, with freedom fighters like young Haliday here, these Red bastards don't have a chance in hell!"

The applause was deafening, and I'd be lying if I didn't say it was also thrilling.

Hooray for young Haliday, the love-blind field agent who, but for a misplaced screwdriver and his own saliva, would be feeding several prosperous hibiscus bushes in a tropical rain forest.

My relationship with my father got better. He married a divorcee named Sally soon after I returned to work. She was nice, had a good sense of humor, and my father worshipped her.

The wedding was held at the swank Chevy Chase Country Club and had lots of high-ranking people in attendance. A young senator from Massachusetts named Jack Kennedy was there.

"He's running for president," my father whispered to me.

I could have cared less, really. I shook the senator's hand and he seemed very thin and sickly. President? I didn't think so.

I cut out early from the reception with my date, a young agency analyst I was seeing at the time.

"Can I ask you a personal question?" she asked as we drove away.

"Fire away," I said.

"Do you like your father?" she said.

"Yes, why?" I asked.

"You seem really quiet around him. Restrained. And his new wife."

"Hmm. I don't mean to be. I need to watch that," I said.

"But do you get along with him?"

"Yes. Now I do. For a while we didn't, but now it's fine. Really."

That new romantic relationship didn't work out too well. Later I started dating Eleanor Wyche, another analyst at the agency. We hit it off well. She didn't seem to mind my odd overseas travel schedule, but then, she was an agency employee and knew the drill.

I asked to be transferred to the Directorate for Plans, where I could live off the glory of my heroic escape and pretty much stay in Washington.

In 1962 Eleanor and I married, and we moved into a house in Alexandria, Virginia. It was a wonderful wedding. My father and Sally were terrific, helping us plan the wedding and offering financial support.

You know, he never really complained about my prior bad attitude toward him; he just let it recede slowly into the background, where it belonged.

In March 1963 my father had his first heart attack. Sally called me at work to give me the news.

I visited him at George Washington University Hospital and was shocked at my reaction. For a guy who had a fraught relationship with his father, I was near tears seeing him in the hospital. After he recuperated, our relationship was never better.

In January 1965 my father died from a massive second heart attack while watching the Jack Benny Show on TV. Eleanor and I rushed over to the hospital, but Sally met us at the emergency room. She was steady and purposeful, describing how father had simply clutched his chest while sipping on his nightly glass of bourbon. She said he uttered nothing and even managed to put his glass down before falling back in his favorite stuffed chair. He stopped breathing instantly and was already dead by the time the ambulance arrived, she said.

Eleanor started crying and hung onto my shoulder as her knees weakened. Sally, who had been strong to this point, also started crying.

And then I started crying. Not little polite sniffles, but big gulping sobs.

There were a lot of reasons for my tears that day, not the least being a smidgen of guilt for being such a selfish, mean-spirited bastard to my father for all those years.

But if I thought that was the end of it, boy, did I have another thing coming.

CHAPTER 38

My father's funeral was held in a small chapel on the grounds of Arlington National Cemetery. During WWII he had reached the rank of Colonel in the Army Air Corps while stationed in England. His will stipulated that he wanted to be buried with full military honors and so he was. I sat with Sally and Eleanor in the front row. In attendance were uncles and aunts from my stepmother and father's sides, as well as my mother Margaret's. And there were a lot of important members of Congress and President Lyndon Johnson's administration.

Eleanor was terrific at keeping me pointed in the right direction. I was such a wreck that she even had to knot my necktie before we left for the funeral.

The service was perfect, at least the part I remember. Uncle Ray, my father's brother, gave a wonderful homily about his life. It was also funny in spots, giving us momentary relief.

The horse-drawn caisson was dramatic, and the ritualized folding of the American flag at the gravesite moved me deeply. I fought to keep myself in control.

At one point during the folding ceremony, my gaze wandered to some of the faces of the mourners. Across the open circle of faces, in the back row, stood a man looking at me. I can't say what drew me to him, but if there are cosmic magnetic forces at work, this was proof of their existence.

He stared at me and I quickly looked away. There were two strange things about this interaction: first, it was an angry look, certainly not the mournful, commiserating look you'd expect at a funeral for your father; second, I had a creepy feeling that I recognized him.

After a few moments, I looked back and just like chimera, the stranger was gone. I wondered if he had just moved into the crowd, or whether my mental health was unraveling, and he had never been there in the first place.

Sally held an open house in McLean. I begged Eleanor to take me home, but she insisted that I attend.

I grabbed a Scotch and water right after walking through the door and tried to hide out in the kitchen, making small talk with one of my cousins while checking my watch every few minutes. Eleanor said I need only stay thirty minutes.

And just like a ghost, the stranger emerged from the milling crowd. He didn't seem to know anyone. I caught him paying his condolences to Sally, who, from the look on her face, had never met him before.

I watched him from across the living room, then lost sight of him in the crush of people. Finally, after twenty-five minutes, I went looking for Eleanor who I'd last seen in the kitchen.

I pushed my way into the crowd there, taking a commiserating slap on the back and kind words from everyone I bumped into.

And there he was again, standing directly in front of me, this little stranger, wearing gray slacks, a blue blazer, and an open-neck, white shirt. He stared at me again with those merciless eyes.

Slowly, the sounds of the room disappeared until it seemed that it was just the two of us standing awkwardly facing each other.

"Do I know you?" I finally said. "You look familiar."

"Sure, don't you remember?" he said, with the faintest foreign accent.

"No, to be honest, I can't."

"Why should you?" he said. "I'd try to forget it too."

After another moment I said, "Who are you?"

"Come on," he said. "You must remember."

This last bit was so strange that it occurred to me he might have been a kook that just wandered off the street at the cemetery. Stranger things have happened.

"Did you know my father?"

"Of course I knew your father," he said. "A great, great man. One of the finest men I knew."

"Well, who are you then?" I repeated, now a little irritated.

"Your father would kill me for talking to you, but, well, he's not around and I couldn't resist meeting you again."

"Again?" I said.

"You know," he said grinning, "we didn't know how long it was going to take you to get out of that damn car trunk. Carlos swore he put the screwdriver back there and Philippe promised me he left plenty of room in the handcuffs for you to slip out. But still, young Mr. Haliday, for a CIA hero, it sure did take you a long time to get out."

Now, for a moment — just a dizzying flash of a moment, mind you — I thought I was hallucinating. My chest prickled with adrenaline and I could feel my palms dampen.

"You were the solo spook in the restaurant!" I said pointing to him.

"Yes, I thought it would come back to you. I've had a lot of strange days in my career, but that was high up there on the list." He made a wistful attempt at a smile, then just looked down at the floor.

"You know, I'm kind of confused right now," I said. "Maybe it's the Scotch, or the funeral, or all of it. But I'm having trouble following you."

"Let's talk," he said. I followed him to the small cocktail bar that was set up in the dining room.

He asked for a beer and I grabbed another Scotch and water. We stood next to each other.

"Would you mind telling me your name?"

"Wilf," he said.

"Wilf who?"

"Just Wilf."

"OK, 'Just Wilf'," I said. "Were you there the night in Panama City that I was kidnapped? Is that how you know so much?"

At this, he chuckled. Then he abruptly stopped, as if remembering something, and grew serious.

"I promised your father. I feel bad I'm breaking my promise, but I think you should know. And what's the harm now, anyway? Was I there that night in Panama? Of course, I was. I kidnapped you."

I grabbed Wilf's wrist and dragged him through the kitchen, onto the deck where there were only a few people.

"What do you mean you kidnapped me? What the hell are you talking about?"

"We kidnapped you. I sat in that stinking little restaurant while you pushed the fat waiter onto me. He almost broke my nose with his elbow, you know."

"No, I didn't know," I said. "Wilf, can you stop beating around the bush. What the hell is going on here? Why did you kidnap me, for god's sake? If that was, in fact, you in the restaurant."

"Why would I make this up? I got better things to do, like honor your father. But he's gone now."

"What did you promise him?"

"That I wouldn't tell you what happened that night. I can't tell you how I met your father or why I knew him. Let's just say he did some important things for me and my family in Puerto Rico. And he called me one night out of the blue and was very upset. He knew what I did for a living and the kind of friends I had. He told me that he had an only child, a son. And that his son worked for the CIA and was in serious trouble in Panama City. That was you."

Incredulous, I said, "Go on."

"He told me that you were in love with some young girl, whose father was an agent for a Soviet Bloc country. He said his son was going to come clean with the girl and her old man, in order to save them. Something like that. Didn't make a bit of sense to me, but I trusted anything your father said. He told me that after divulging your real identity and warning them of something bad, you were supposed to go right to the Canal Zone and stay safe on US soil."

"Yeah, so why did he need to call you?" I said.

"Ah, yes. He said he didn't believe you were going to do that. He had a feeling you were going to try to see the girl again."

"He told you that?"

"And he was right, too."

"So, you tailed me?"

"Yep, just like he said, to your little love bird. But you didn't know she was being tailed too."

"Let me get this — my father sent you to protect me?"

"Not just protect. He said if there was any trouble, we were to grab you and make it seem like we were the bad guys. Then we were to let you escape somehow to the Canal Zone. It was Carlos who thought of the trunk idea. He said any monkey can get out of a car trunk with a screwdriver. Christ, though, I thought we were going to run out of gas before you got out of that damn car."

I walked away from Wilf and over to an Adirondack chair. I sat down and looked back warily at him.

"I don't believe you," I said.

"Your father said it had to look like you got away from us by yourself. He said if you knew he had tried to help you, that you'd never forgive him. He said you did not like him much, but he still loved you."

"I don't believe you," I said again, with less conviction.

"That's OK. Doesn't bother me," Wilf said. "You know, he paid us a lot of money to do this trip. We almost missed the flight from San Juan. It was close."

"How did you meet my father?" I asked.

"None of your business."

"How do I know you're not making all this up?"

He laughed. "I gather you and your father reconciled later and got along great. But when you were in Panama, he said you hated him. Or something like that. And I promised never to tell you. He said you'd never forgive him. What kind of beef did you have with your father that made him act this way?"

I stared at the back yard.

"Families struggle at times. What can I say? I'm not proud of it, but there you are."

"Well, nice meeting you," he said.

"Hey, Wilf. Wait."

He stopped and turned.

"There were two goons that night. They chased me down the alley."

"You bet and I almost had a heart attack. One of those little bastards opened up on you and I thought he put a slug through your skull."

"So, what happened to them?"

"Who?" he said.

"The two goons."

"Oh. I killed them."

Wilf turned and walked away. I sat in the chair, staring at two forlorn white birch trees in the yard. I sipped my drink until it was just ice, then I methodically chewed the ice. It could have been thirty minutes or two hours. Finally, Eleanor found me.

"Good lord, Nick," she said. "How long have you been out here? I couldn't find you anywhere."

"Can we go home now," I said. "I have a headache."

"Sure," she said rubbing the back of my neck. "You poor thing."

CHAPTER 39

It took me a while to get my bearings in life after the funeral. Eleanor thought I needed to see a psychiatrist, but I refused.

And, tormented with guilt toward my father, and feeling a good dose of shame for my sham award at the agency, I asked for a transfer back to the Operations Directorate.

My boss, a short, balding fellow named Stan, told me to forget about it. "They're not going to let you back in Operations. They have plenty of goons out there. You've paid your dues."

I insisted, of course, and after more than a year waiting, they took me back in. Eleanor was beside herself. She had just given birth to our daughter Francine, and she knew what the assignments were like in the clandestine service.

"This is incredibly self-destructive," she yelled at me one night. "You're going back to a dangerous line of work. And you're leaving us all alone. It doesn't make sense, Nick."

I told her I had no choice, and I didn't really. Guilt and self-loathing are powerful forces that only death can stop.

They sent me back to Camp Peary for retraining, and I hated every second of it. Seymour was still there, and he kept pointing me out to the class as an example of good training and brilliant fieldwork. I made him promise privately never to mention my exploits again. He took it as abject piety on my part and treated me with near religious deference afterwards.

And then back to Washington where I waited for assignment.

Eleanor, our daughter Francine, and I lived a happy life during this period. The cherry blossoms bloomed early in April and we pushed little Franny's carriage around the Tidal Pool. The petals fell like huge pink snowflakes and we laughed as we kept brushing them off her blanket. We couldn't have been happier, and it was only proper I suppose, that there was a calm before the storm.

In the fall of 1965, I got my marching orders. President Lyndon Johnson had decided to escalate a conflict in a country called Vietnam, and that's where they sent a large contingent of field agents.

From 1966 through 1969 — with several RR rotations back home — I worked in Southeast Asia: two years in Saigon, one in in Bangkok. Our son Alexander was conceived on one of those RR trips to Honolulu.

I did many bad things for my country. I'm haunted to this day by several episodes, one involving an entire South Vietnamese family, including children. In my wildest dreams, I never believed life could be so cheap — and cruel. I returned from Southeast Asia in 1969 a forlorn, rattled man.

Eleanor said I drank and smoked too much; I had taken up cigarettes. I had also smoked a lot of pot and even some opium when I was in country.

Adjusting to the relative quiet and safety of Alexandria, Virginia, was more difficult than I anticipated. My daughter Franny and our son Alex were bright points in my life, and I thrilled to take them to the playground.

About three months after my return I had a powerful dream.

It was about Maria.

To be fair, I had dreamed about Maria off and on over the years.

In these other dreams, she made a fleeting entry and exit, often at the gauzy periphery of the main stage. These dreams stirred nothing in me.

But this new dream was different. Maria was front and center. She looked like she did the night we last saw each other: a long brightly colored print skirt and short-sleeve white cotton blouse. Her long dark brown hair was pulled back with a yellow plastic headband. We held hands like silly kids and gazed into each other's eyes. It was the innocent time — before the kidnapping, the false award, my father's passing, and my hell in Southeast Asia.

In the dream, Maria sported that proud, independent, and vulnerable smile. She uttered only three words: "I miss you."

Not much of a dream, really. But it moved me with a profound intensity I couldn't contain. It lurked back there in my consciousness the rest of the week.

That weekend I called a fellow warrior at the agency and asked him how I could track the whereabouts of someone I'd known eleven years ago.

"Oh great, an old girlfriend," he said. "Forget it, man. We don't encourage stalkers."

"Come on, Steve, it's important. You must know someone who could do this for me."

"Where does she live?" he said.

"Last time I saw her was in Panama City."

"Panama City, Florida. OK, it's a start."

"No, Panama City, Panama."

"Oh shit, Nick, this isn't a person involved in that old mission of yours? The one that you got that award for, is it?"

"Maybe, maybe not."

"Do yourself one huge goddamn favor, Nick — drop this. Don't go tracking over old territory. You were on assignment for an agency of the United States government. You're not authorized to re-contact any of these people. Jeeze, Nick, all you guys back from Nam are absolutely fucked in the head."

"You going to help or not?"

There was a pause. "I'm going to help because I feel sorry for you, you stupid shit. Have they talked to you about seeing a shrink? They'll pay for everything. It's confidential."

"Are you going to help?"

"God! All right. Let me get a pen."

I told him everything I could remember — times, addresses, names, the works.

"It'll cost you," he told me, "even if they can't find anything."

"Doesn't matter. See what they come up with."

My interest in tracking down Maria waned. But Steve called back six days later.

"OK, it'll cost you $5,000 for this stuff, and I'm not fronting for you so you need to promise you'll pay up."

"You know I'm good for it."

"OK, this Maria Santiago, she's no longer in Panama, that's for sure. If they got the right one, she lives in Cuba."

"Cuba? You've got to be kidding me," I said.

"Hell, I don't know. I'm just reading to you what I got. You want more?"

"Yeah, go on."

"OK, says here that her family fled to Cuba in the late 1950s and took up with Fidel and his band of merry guerillas. When Fidel took over in 1959, Maria's dad was made the minister of agriculture. Maria married a party functionary named Ramon Chavez. They live outside Havana. They have two kids."

"Do you know where they live? Do you have an address?"

"Why, do you want to send her a love letter?"

"Just give me the address."

"Are you going to pay up for this stuff?"

"I gave you my word, Steve."

"I've got to be honest with you Nick, you're kind of freaking me out with all this shit. Give it a rest."

"Give me the address."

CHAPTER 40

I left Eleanor, Franny, and Alex on a Friday afternoon and drove to Dulles. As far as she was concerned, I was on business. The flight to London was half full and I did my best to sleep, but I was nervous.

It was a wild trajectory I was on, racing across the sky to do something that was insane and dangerous. But there really was no stopping me. I was determined to find something that had been lost a while ago.

As strange as this sounds, I still loved Eleanor; she had coaxed me through so much turmoil and was a terrific partner and mother. How could I ask for more?

But I was *crazy*. I needed to find Maria and I couldn't control myself. Maria held the key to something that I couldn't articulate.

I stayed in London for a couple of days, practicing my cover, and making sure everything was clean in my suitcase.

I was only in Amsterdam long enough to get a drink at the airport bar, then I was on to Cuba. My impeccable fake passport — from another spurious friend — passed muster in The Netherlands, which was a good walk-through for Havana.

Pretending to be Tom Hardy, a visiting Canadian free-lance journalist, I had arranged several interviews over my three days there. My journalistic angle was the high quality of Cuban medicine, and they

KEITH YOCUM

were thrilled to show off their universal health care.

The DGI — Cuban Secret Police — are no fools. They'd salivate to get their hands on a crazed CIA agent who was way off the reservation.

Putting on my best earnest Canadian look, and packing a flawless Canadian passport and Cuban visa, I breezed through the airport and found myself unpacking in my room at the Ambos Mundos Hotel in Old Havana. The place was crawling with Russians, so I pretty much kept to myself.

Like all visiting journalists, I had been appointed an interpreter/babysitter/spy to be my intermediary. Her name was Louisa, and she was short, stocky, and strikingly pleasant. We got along famously. At my first two interviews — the director of a children's clinic in downtown Havana and the Secretariat of Health at government offices — had gone well, I thought. I had thoroughly prepped myself for the subject.

Before leaving on this escapade, I had paid a handsome sum to a former agency contractor I knew in Miami who had contacts in Cuba. He supposedly scouted out my subject, but to be honest, I wasn't sure about anything. According to the contractor, Maria's schedule was fairly regular, and she liked to go food shopping at a particular grocery store on Tuesday afternoons at around 1 p.m. The grocery store was only three-quarters of a mile from the hotel.

Tuesday morning Louisa and the driver picked me up for my last interview with an extraordinarily boring surgeon at Havana's main hospital. It lasted two hours. Louisa asked if she could arrange any additional interviews for me. I told her I didn't think so. I said I was exhausted and would probably sleep for the rest of the afternoon.

I had lunch in the hotel's outdoor café, then yawned heavily and returned to my room. I quickly threw on an incredibly distressed pair of shorts, a slightly torn once-white cotton t-shirt, a pair of old sneakers, and a distressed straw hat.

I walked all the way to the ground floor using the stairway and slung a cotton carry bag over my shoulder. Using the Caribbean "saunter," a languorous walking gait that suggested I had nowhere to go, it took twenty minutes to reach the small grocery store.

I scanned the lot for her car, a dark blue Moskvich-408, but couldn't find it. I loitered in the small vegetable section inside, examining nearly every single mango, breadfruit, and avocado until I felt compelled to move to the papayas.

At 1:10 doubt began to creep in. After coming this far and rashly offering myself up to the KGB and DGI, it occurred to me that some mundane event — a sick child, a flat tire, a headache — was going to prevent me from seeing Maria. Perhaps it was meant to be this way.

At 1:25 I became concerned that my presence in the small store was being noticed. Oddity and peculiar behavior are dangerous in a police state. The cashier began to watch me. I'm sure he perceived a vague foreignness about me.

The disappointment of missing Maria was offset now by the recognition of how stupidly rash I had been. I was ripped with fear and raced out of the store and into the sunlight.

Holding up my hand for protection from the glare and squinting, I nearly knocked someone over and kept going across the parking lot.

And there was the little blue 408. I swooned and found a small group of trees to wait under. It occurred to me that I had probably bumped into her on my way out.

Perhaps thirty minutes passed before she came out carrying two mesh bags of groceries. I watched her struggle toward her car and marveled at how beautiful she was. She wore a light brown cotton sleeveless dress. Her hair was cut short, and she wore a pair of stylish sunglasses. She had put on just a little weight, and her strong arms tensed as she balanced her grocery bags and wrestled them onto the floor of the backseat of her car.

By the time she was behind the wheel, I had opened the front passenger door and leaned in.

She looked up at me, and in a harshly dismissive tone, yelled at me in Spanish, presumably, to get the hell out of her car.

"Maria," I said.

She stopped and turned her head to get a better look at me. Then her lower jaw nearly fell off. She screamed sharply and jumped about an inch off the seat. I could not see her eyes through the sunglasses, but she froze with both hands to her mouth.

"Maria, it's Nick."

She yelped and jumped again, this time not so loudly, which I was happy about. I quickly shot a glance into the grocery store over the roof of the car, and then leaned back in.

"Hi, Maria. I'm sorry I scared you. I didn't know how to do this and figured this would be less surprising. Guess I was wrong."

She just stared at me, the fingers of both hands curled back on her bottom lip and exposed teeth as if they were piano keys.

"Do you mind if I sit in your car? It would draw less attention."

She stared.

"Maria," I repeated. "Is it OK to sit?"

Nothing.

I decided to sit down anyway. I closed the door behind me and wound down the window.

I turned to look at her, and after rehearsing a million times what I would say, it all evaporated into thin air. Maria remained frozen, fingertips in her mouth, breathing heavily, while I tried to engage her.

"Maria, I know this seems kind of crazy — no, not *seems* crazy — *is* crazy. But I really had to see you. And I've come a long way to do it, as you can probably guess."

More silence.

"Damn," I said looking out the window into the gravel parking lot, "I practiced everything I wanted to say. Now I don't know what the heck I'm doing."

"What are you doing here?" she whispered.

"I don't know, really. I just came to see you," I said, thankful she finally said something. "I miss you."

"You *miss* me?" she said. "Nick, it has been a very long time. How can you miss me?" Her accent was stronger, and I had difficulty understanding her.

The words "I miss you," weren't exactly what I had in mind. It sounded so trite and didn't express what was going through my troubled head.

"I thought you were dead, Nick," she said. "You are like a ghost. You are making me very confused."

"I'm alive. Look, pinch me," I said holding up my forearm.

She refused to touch me.

"OK, let me try again. Maria," I said. "It may sound completely outlandish to you—-"

"What is 'outlandish'?" she interrupted.

"Crazy," I said. "Although it's been a long time, I've thought about you a lot. Lately, it seems that you're all that I can think about."

"Talk slow," she said, "I do not understand you so well."

I laughed. I had traveled halfway around the world, on this penitential pilgrimage to my long-lost innocent love, and she couldn't understand what I was saying.

I sighed, chuckled again, and stared out through the windshield. A car pulled into the parking lot, and the sound of the crunching gravel seemed a hundred times louder than it should have. Two older men got out, laughing about something they had just shared.

There was silence again as I struggled to say something meaningful, and Maria watched this lunatic who had invaded her car.

"Actually," I said looking straight ahead, "I shouldn't have scared you like this. You see what happens to burned out spies? Nothing good at all happens to them."

"You are still a spy?" she said.

I considered lying, of course, but at this point, I was so disgusted and low that it was too late.

"Yep. American spy. CIA operative. Defender of Freedom."

"Nick, how did you get here? To Cuba?"

I laughed derisively. "I'm pretending to be a Canadian journalist."

"You are now spying on Cuba? On me? My husband?"

"Whoa," I said turning. "No, Maria. I'm not spying on you or anyone here. This is my third day; I'm leaving tomorrow. My country doesn't know I'm here."

"You are confusing to me, Nick. Why did you come to Cuba?"

"To find you."

"Me? But that is silly — and very dangerous. Dangerous for me, and my family."

"Yes, I know that, and I should have thought of how bad it could be for you. Shows you how nutty I am."

"What is 'nutty'"?

"*Loco.* I'm *loco,* Maria."

"But why did you come, Nick?"

"To see you again. I couldn't get you out of my mind. Yes, I know it sounds absolutely insane that I would do something like this, but there it is. I wanted to see you again. Maria, I was so in love with you years ago and nothing has come close to that feeling since. It's that simple."

"You should not have come, Nick. It was a long time ago. We are different people." At this, she quickly looked around the parking lot.

"Yes, I realize that now," I said, looking out the windshield again. "But Maria, I can't tell you how much I have missed you all those years. You're such a special person. I don't think you've stopped being a special person to me."

"How can you say that? You do not know me."

"Because you can't change what's part of your nature, Maria. It's not possible. And you're as beautiful as when I last saw you."

There was silence again in the car. Maria had dropped her hands into her lap, and slowly raised her right hand and took off her sunglasses. I got a chance to look into those sparkling hazel eyes again and they were as bright as the last time I saw them.

"Please do not say those things, Nick."

"Why? It's true. You look great."

"Ha," she said. "You are just like the old Nick."

"Well, let me ask you," I said. "Did you ever think of me? Didn't you at least wonder what I was doing?"

"But I thought you were dead."

"Didn't you ever wonder what it would have been like if we had escaped together? We would have made a terrific couple. You must admit that. Come on, you must have imagined that."

"Nick, you are so confusing to me."

"Maria, I'm asking you straight — did you ever wonder what it would have been like if we had stayed together?"

"OK, yes, but that was a long time ago."

"Well, that feeling that you had a long time ago, I have now. And it won't leave me alone. You've dragged me from Virginia to Cuba."

"I did not drag you."

"Of course, you did. I'm here now."

"Nick! Please stop. What do you want? I don't understand."

"I don't know what I want."

"Nick, now you are driving me crazy! Aiy." She raised both her hands to the side of her face and turned to look out the front of the car again. She sighed.

"Eleanor will have me committed if she knew where I was. This is what happens to old spies. They either play golf or they go crazy."

"Who is Eleanor?" she said.

"My wife. A good person."

"Children?"

"Yes. Two"

"What is their names?"

"Francine and Alex."

"Good names."

"And I know you're married. What is his name?"

"Rafael."

"And you have two boys, I know that much."

"You are a good spy."

"What are their names?"

"Phillipe," she said.

"And the other?"

She hesitated. "Nicholai," she said.

"Ah," I said turning to face her in the hot car. "See. You were thinking of me."

"But Nick, you were dead."

"I'm not dead now."

"Aiy, you make me so nervous, Nick. You must go."

"So you really thought of me?"

"Yes, I have thought of you. But you were a memory. Now you are real. Aiy."

And, as if she had been stung by a bee, she sat up, put on her sunglasses, and bit the inside of her lip in the way I remembered.

"You must go, Nick. I am too nervous around you. Go now." She reached over and turned on the ignition.

"Can I ask one small favor?"

"What is your favor?"

"Can I kiss you goodbye?"

"No. That would not be good, Nick. Please do not try to kiss me." She sighed again.

I opened the door and got out. Leaning back in I said, "Can I leave you something? It's very small."

She looked at me suspiciously.

Without waiting for her response, I threw the tiny strip of paper onto the passenger seat. She looked at it, reached over, picked it up and held it about six inches from her face. I couldn't read her expression because of the sunglasses.

She held it there motionless while her car idled. I waited for her to say something, but she didn't move. And right before I started to speak, something large hit her blouse with a plop. Following its trajectory, I saw it was a teardrop that had slid from underneath the dark-green lens.

"Maria," I said, "I know it was a long time ago, and we're older. But something special happened in Panama. Do we just let it go? I don't know. I guess we do."

She didn't move nor respond to me, she simply kept looking at the black-and-white photo strip we had taken that day in May 1958 in a Panama City drug store. The fourth one was my favorite photo: I had my arm around Maria, and she was nuzzled upwards, against my cheek, just staring with that little half smile of hers. And I looked down on her raised face, at peace, and foolishly, madly in love.

Getting out of Cuba went as planned. The trip was so audacious that no one suspected. Not the CIA, GRI, KGB, or even Eleanor. In fact, sitting in my kitchen later that week in Alexandria, Virginia, I wondered if it had really happened.

And I'm going on with life. I have renewed enthusiasm for my work, though I'm back in Planning again. Eleanor, Franny, Alex and I are a happy suburban family.

I still think of Maria. She is a small shining star in a vast, dark galaxy that I cannot stop looking at.

There are forces at work in this insanely complicated universe that I do not understand. I didn't make the rules; hell, I don't even understand the rules. The fact is, there was something lost, and then something else was found. Perhaps that's all that matters.

Perhaps.

EPILOGUE

Haliday's children and their lawyer attempted to contact individuals mentioned in his memoir. Because of the redactions made by the agency, it was impossible to find most of them.

One name they were able to trace was Maria Chavez, who lived in Cuba. Due to more relaxed relations between the two countries, they were able to find Maria's address and wrote her a letter. They identified themselves, made a brief introduction, and mentioned that their father had passed away in 2008. They also said that he had left a memoir in which he detailed a relationship with her.

Maria wrote back to them. The letter was short, thanking them for connecting with her:

"Your father was a good man. I'm sure he is happy in heaven now. We knew each other many years ago. We were very young. I liked him very much. I sometimes dream of him still. I am sorry to say I am sick now, with cancer, so my thoughts are not so clear. Be proud of your father. He was a brave and very passionate man. Please accept my gift to you of three small photographs of your father and me taken a very long time ago. I have kept three other photos for my own children. May God be with him."

Maria Chavez passed away in Havana in 2018 at age 81.

AUTHOR'S NOTE

Miraflores — Memoir of a Young Spy is a work of fiction woven around actual events in Panama and the Canal Zone in 1958.

Those events also affected my family, which was living in the Canal Zone at the time. I was a second grade student at Ancon Elementary School during the May 1958 riots and was one of many students accidentally teargassed. My father, Edward Yocum, also took 8mm film of the riots, which I reviewed extensively in researching the book. I visited the US National Archives and Records Administration to review newspaper articles from the now-defunct Panama City-based *Star & Herald*. I also visited Panama and toured the University of Panama, including some classrooms that were in use in 1958.

I took liberties with the timing of events in May 1958 but left the main occurrences intact. For instance, there was an Operation Sovereignty in which Panamanian students planted their national flag throughout the Canal Zone. There was indeed seething anger felt by many Panamanians at compensation policies that paid American employees of the canal a higher wage than Panamanians doing similar work.

The May 1958 riots in Panama City left eight people dead and were aimed ostensibly at the Panamanian government around educational reform and funding. There was also an undercurrent of anti-Americanism. Students at the University of Panama played a key part in the resistance.

While the riots depicted in this novel were factual, other narrative elements like Operation Banyan Tree are entirely fictional. The characters of Nick Halliday, Maria Santiago, and their families are fictional. There is no evidence that leaders of the Panamanian opposition in 1958 were targeted with assassination by the US intelligence services.

The riots in 1958 occurred against a backdrop of nationalism and resistance against entrenched ruling families and military juntas throughout South and Central America. Some of the resistance was encouraged and abetted by communist organizations.

During this period, Western governments engaged in a vigorous international policy of containment against the perceived threat of communist expansion, with many overt and covert programs that were the basis of countless Cold War-era espionage activities.

In 1977 President Jimmy Carter was a signatory to the Torrijos-Carter Treaty, which started the process of returning the canal to Panamanian control. US withdrawal was completed on December 31, 1999.

MORE FROM KEITH YOCUM

Color of Blood

(Book 1 of the Dennis Cunningham series)

Dennis is glad to be back at work. His wife's death left him devastated but he'll do anything to lose himself into work at the Inspector General's office of the CIA. A brilliant, if prickly investigator, he's spent his career chasing down the Agency's thieves and liars. When his boss forces him to take a low-level assignment to investigate a missing employee in Australia, he soon finds that even in the red dust of the Outback, there is romance – and death – just a sweltering heartbeat away.

A Dark Place

(Book 2 of the Dennis Cunningham series)

An old case spills new blood. Dennis loves policing the CIA's network of spies for liars and thieves. But each time he plows into a case, it's harder for him to keep alive his relationship with Judy, an Aussie cop and the only woman who understands his passions and quirks. When Dennis and Judy meet in London to rekindle their relationship, they are sucked into the city's dark underworld. To save Judy's life Dennis must solve two cases simultaneously. If you like non-stop action, dark humor and complicated heroes, then you'll love *A Dark Place*.

Valley of Spies

(BOOK 3 OF THE DENNIS CUNNINGHAM SERIES)

When an American woman vanishes in New Zealand, it perplexes authorities. There is no body, no witness and no motive. But what looks like a sad, unfortunate case of foul play, slowly turns into something darker. The missing tourist is a female psychologist under contract from the CIA to see employees in strictest confidence. Was her disappearance a random act of violence, or an act of international espionage? Does someone want to know her patients' dark, dirty secrets? Dennis Cunningham, the gruff but uncanny CIA investigator, is tugged out of early retirement in Western Australia to rubber stamp a foregone conclusion by the agency about the real perpetrators. A brilliant but unusual sleuth, Cunningham can't help but pick at the agency's scab on this case until it bleeds red all over.

Daniel

STRANGE THINGS HAPPEN IN WAR –
BUT VIETNAM WAS ALWAYS DIFFERENT

In January 1972, during the waning days of that sad war, a lone soldier crawled through the barbed wire and entered an isolated American firebase. He said his name was Daniel Carson, but a quick check found that a soldier with the same name and physical description was already buried at Arlington National Cemetery. Who was this new soldier named Daniel? Was he a crazy man, a common deserter or something else entirely? And why did he have such a profound effect on the unlucky company of grunts trying to survive the last days of the war? As a fierce regiment of North Vietnamese regulars prepares to destroy the forgotten hilltop firebase, the odd little soldier named Daniel seems to have all the answers to their survival. Several years after the war, three survivors of the firebase meet in Washington, D.C. and, almost by accident, discover the shocking truth about Daniel.

Titus

IN THE MIDST OF CARNAGE IN THE CIVIL WAR,
IS THERE A SERIAL MURDERER AT WORK?

A Union soldier is found dead on the outskirts of camp, his neck sliced open from ear to ear. But when more soldiers are found with their throats slit, an uneasy mood falls over the Union regiment. Who is killing these soldiers, and what does the strange mark on the dead men's foreheads mean? A young Union lieutenant and an eccentric field surgeon are ordered to get to the bottom of the killings. Can the two officers unmask the killer and motive before the fog of battle hides his identity forever?

KEITH YOCUM lives on Cape Cod. He has worked for *The Boston Globe* and *The New England Journal of Medicine.* He is the author of six novels and welcomes feedback at www.keithyocum.com.